iPads
in the
Classroom

iPads
in the
Classroom

From Consumption and
Curation to Creation

TOM DACCORD & JUSTIN REICH

LEARNING AND PERFORMANCE MANAGEMENT

1400 Centrepark Blvd, Suite 1000
West Palm Beach, FL 33401
717-845-6300

email: pub@learningsciences.com
learningsciences.com

Printed in the United States of America

20 19 18 17 16 15   1 2 3 4 5 6

Publisher's Cataloging-in-Publication Data

Daccord, Tom.
  iPads in the classroom / Tom Daccord [and] Justin Reich.
pages cm
ISBN: 978-1-941112-93-9 (pbk.)
  1. iPad (Computer) 2. Tablet computers. 3. Educational technology. 4. Education—Effect of technological innovations on. 5. Teaching—Aids and devices.   I. Reich, Justin, 1977- II. Title.
LB1028.43 .D33 2015
371.33`4—dc23

Table of Contents

Acknowledgments

Learning Sciences International would like to thank the following reviewers:

Elizabeth F. Day
2005 New York Teacher of the Year
Mechanicville Middle School
Mechanicville, New York

Michael Funkhouser
2013 West Virginia Teacher of the Year
East Hardy High School
Baker, West Virginia

Anne E. Hasse
2014 Wisconsin Elementary Teacher
   of the Year
Wakanda Elementary School
Menomonie, Wisconsin

Wanda Lacy
2013 Tennessee Teacher of the Year
Farragut High School
Knoxville, Tennessee

Yung Romano
2010 Alabama Teacher of the Year
Strawberry Crest High School
Dover, Florida

Aaron Sitze
2013 Illinois Teacher of the Year finalist
Oregon High School
Oregon, Illinois

James L. Smith
2003 New Mexico Teacher of the Year
Mayfield High School
Las Cruces, New Mexico

Kathleen Turner
2013 Massachusetts Teacher of the Year
Sharon High School
Sharon, Massachusetts

About the Authors

Tom Daccord is director and cofounder of EdTechTeacher. An educational technology speaker, instructor, and author, Tom has worked with schools, districts, colleges, and educational organizations in the United States, Canada, Europe, Asia, and the Middle East. He has presented on educational technology topics at national and international conferences, including at the International Society for Technology in Education Conference (United States), the Florida Education Technology Conference (United States), the European League for Middle Level Education Conference (Europe), the International Conference on Teaching and Learning with Technology (Asia), and the Near East South Asia Council of Overseas Schools Spring Educators Conference (Asia). He has also organized a series of sold-out international EdTechTeacher iPad Summits in the United States. Tom has also produced a series of online courses on Web 2.0 and iPad integration as well as 21st century school leadership and classroom assessment.

Justin Reich is the executive director of the MIT Teaching Systems Lab, where he investigates the technology-rich classrooms of the future and the systems we need to prepare teachers to thrive in those classrooms. Justin is also a fellow at the Berkman Center for Internet and Society, a visiting lecturer in the Scheller Teacher Education Program at MIT, and the cofounder of EdTechTeacher, a professional learning consultancy devoted to helping teachers leverage technology to create student-centered, inquiry-based learning environments.

Introduction

If Eddie had just submitted the answer on a worksheet, his teacher, Jennie Magiera, would have simply marked it wrong and moved on with her grading.

The question was, "Which bag of cheese is the better value?" Eddie's answer was not missed-a-decimal-point wrong or forgot-the-negative-sign wrong; it was off-the-wall, how-could-you-possibly-come-up-with-that wrong. His answer was "$16."

Just like many of Jennie's students in the urban heart of Chicago, Eddie was a bright child from a challenging home environment. And as much as the fourth-grade teacher loved all of her students equally, some tried her patience more than others.

Fortunately, Eddie did not turn in this assignment on a worksheet. He submitted his answer through Google Forms, along with a link to a screencast of himself working through the problem, created by using the Explain Everything app on his iPad. When Jennie saw the bizarre answer that Eddie had turned in, she was able to pull his video out of her Dropbox folder and view the process that led to his incorrect submission.

Jennie's class was working on ratios and proportions, so on a recent grocery trip she had used her smartphone to make a short video from the dairy aisle in which she showed students several different products with competing sizes and prices. She then projected the video in class and asked the students to use the data from the video to create and solve their own unique math problems. Since Eddie had created the question himself, it was very strange that he would come up with such an off-the-wall answer. It was lucky for Eddie that Jennie had also instructed her students to use the screencasting app to both write out their process and talk it through out loud.

As soon as Eddie's video started, Jennie realized that he had decided to round all the x.99 prices to an even dollar amount to simplify the task. He was one of only two students out of ninety-seven to use that sensible strategy, which was one reason that his answer looked different from the ones submitted by his peers. Jennie watched further into the video as Eddie talked through his strategy, and after about forty-five seconds, she noticed that he made a simple but critical error: when moving his calculations from one "digital sheet" of paper to another, he transposed a number from an earlier step in his calculations rather than the last step. Oops. In the end, Eddie forgot the original question he had set up for himself and ended up solving the question of how much it would cost to buy four small bags of cheese rather than which bag was the better value.

As strange as his answer seemed, Jennie saw that nearly every mathematical move that Eddie made in his calculations was correct; he just forgot his original question and made one transposition error. Since Eddie had produced a record of his work and learning, Jennie was able to gain an understanding of the incorrect details in his performance that would have been lost in a simple fill-in-the-blank worksheet. Jennie did not score the question at all on Eddie's submission form. What she did next is brilliant.

Instead of handing Eddie a grade of *0* or directly explaining to him what he had done wrong, Jennie just told him to get his iPad and watch his own screencast. Thirty seconds into watching himself solve the problem, Eddie let out an audible groan, as he heard himself talk aloud through the mistake he had made. He smiled at his teacher, explained his mistake, and asked if he could correct it. And, of course, Jennie let him fix his mistake and get it right.

The Surge of iPads in Schools

Jennie told this story during her keynote address at the second EdTechTeacher iPad Summit in Atlanta. She had gotten into teaching because of her love for math and kids, but early in her career she approached technology with a great deal of skepticism. What, she wondered, do computers or cell phones or tablets have to do with getting kids to understand (or even love) math?

After years of slowly incorporating digital tools into her teaching, though, she came to believe that mobile technologies had a tremendous potential to bring real-world dilemmas into the classroom. Students would thereby be enabled to gain more ownership over their learning and create performances of understanding that demonstrated learning in powerful ways to teachers, to peers, and—most importantly—to themselves. The once-tech-averse, tech-anxious Jennie Magiera is now the digital learning coordinator for the Academy for Urban School Leadership in Chicago and a sought-after speaker and professional development trainer.

Jennie and her colleagues at the academy are not alone in bringing iPads into their classrooms. Over 10 million iPads have been purchased for educational settings all over the world. Tens of thousands of classroom teachers and students in the United States are now using iPads for learning. Urban school districts have made large-scale purchases of iPads, and countless suburban and rural schools have also initiated programs related to the technology.

The speed of adoption of these devices is astonishing, exciting, and terrifying.

It is astonishing that a technology platform—the tablet—with basically no traction at all in schools could be adopted so quickly and that so many school boards, district officials, and independent school trustee boards would choose to invest in the device so rapidly.

It is exciting that hundreds of schools that had watched and waited as other schools experimented with one-to-one laptop programs were willing to take advantage of the lower costs and higher prestige of the fancy new iPads and invest in getting an Internet-connected device in the hands of every learner.

It is terrifying, because no one knew how to use these devices—designed for watching movies and reading magazines in your lap—for teaching and learning with kids.

It is also encouraging because the history of educational technology adoption around the world is not a confidence-inspiring one. While there have always been extraordinary teachers like Jennie Magiera, who have leveraged new technologies to create incredibly rich learning experiences for students, for the most part teachers have used technology to extend existing practices. In the early years of using personal computers in schools, for example, teachers transfer notes from acetate sheets for overhead projectors to PowerPoint slides at great cost but without much gain.

Placing millions of iPads in the hands of students has suddenly created an opportunity for us to rethink and redesign learning. iPads bring possibilities for mobile, differentiated, and personalized learning, which, to this point, was unimaginable in many American schools. By providing multiple pathways for student learning, teachers can use iPads to reshape physical and virtual learning environments for students. iPads can be used to help students access content at a level and pace best suited to their individual development. Kinesthetic elements of the iPad allow for new and innovative exploration of educational content—be it a molecule, a painting, a map, or any of the other teaching devices—that goes well beyond the affordances of pen and paper. iPads also enable teachers and students to interact with educational resources (and one another) in innovative ways that surpass the limitations of many traditional classrooms. Most important, the new possibilities inspired by the presence of this new tool in today's classrooms provide a tremendous opportunity for educators to rethink the design of learning environments in ways that will best suit the needs of today's students.

We are in the midst of a moment that does not come often: the widespread adoption of a device that has the potential to open people's minds to what technology can make possible in education. As a nation, we have not done a great job of redefining learning during our experiments with computer labs and interactive whiteboards. This is our chance for a reboot, a chance to put learning and vision at the heart of the adoption of a new technology.

Yet, despite the incredible influx of iPads in our classrooms, this opportunity to craft purposeful and meaningful learning is being lost. Many middle and high schools are using iPads exclusively as replacements for notebooks and textbooks. Many elementary schools are using them as game stations to simply keep students who race ahead or cause trouble occupied. Most schools are overlooking the mobile, personalized learning opportunities made possible with iPads and instead incorporating them in ill-suited, teacher-centric learning environments. Many educators are too focused on the conveniences and allure of iPads and are pushing ahead to discuss purchase plans, app selection, and device distribution, before first developing a vision of effective student learning with the devices.

Technology in the Service of Learning

In all of EdTechTeacher's work, our first principle is a simple one: technology needs to be in the service of learning. This may seem obvious, but all too often technology becomes an end unto itself, rather than a coherent part of a community plan for learning. For example, in our home state of Massachusetts, each district is required to submit a technology plan—describing purchase plans, maintenance, and sustainability—yet nowhere in that plan does the district need to describe how its strategies will advance learning.

At a recent conference where we were part of a panel discussing iPads, the moderator asked the question, "Why should a school or district choose to invest in iPads?" An IT director started his answer by saying that iPads had a long battery life and there would not be cords all over the room when students were working. While we are all for workplace safety, educational technology decisions should not be driven by the presence or absence of power cords. We should be talking about helping young people have a meaningful, engaging, empowering education.

Since 2004, we at EdTechTeacher have been working with schools and districts to help them use emerging technologies to create student-centered, inquiry-based learning environments. We have always been device and platform agnostic. We believe that a holistic education for young people in the digital age requires giving them access to the digital tools needed to access new forms of knowledge, to personalize their studies, to connect with people around the world, and to demonstrate their understandings in diverse ways. We think educators can enable this access using all kinds of devices and platforms. Choosing the best tools is important but not as important as supporting teachers in incorporating technology in thoughtful ways that will empower students.

We feel that the real focus of any technology integration should not be the tool but rather a clear vision and pedagogy. The fundamental questions every school buying iPads needs to answer are: Why iPads? How, exactly, does an iPad align with a vision of meaningful and purposeful learning?

In 2012, we started seeing schools and districts making major investments in iPads, and we started hearing those same schools ask for help in supporting their teachers in incorporating these new devices into their classrooms. Those early adopters have been joined by other schools at an incredibly rapid pace. Since then, we at EdTechTeacher have made a major effort to study the practices of the best early adopters and examine their successes and challenges. We partnered with districts to create full-year blended learning K–12 iPad integration programs to investigate and support pioneering districts in iPad adoption. We also have convened gatherings of innovative iPad-using educators at a series of iPad Summits, held in Boston, Atlanta, and San Diego. One of the first magazine articles that came out about our iPad summit was: "The iPads in Education Conference That's Not About iPads" (Forston, 2013). We loved the title. We will admit it: the conference headline was a trick to get those people who started off thinking they were merely interested in iPads really interested in great teaching and learning that takes advantage of iPads.

We'll also admit the title of this book is a trick, too. If we do our job in the pages ahead, we will be talking about creating powerful learning environments with iPads just as much as we are talking about the device and its apps.

So, if you were hoping this book was going to tell you about the ten must-have, game-changer apps to transform your classroom, we are sorry to disappoint. There are no must-have apps for every classroom. Every conversation about technology needs to start with the questions: What do you want your kids to be able to do when they leave your classroom, your grade, your building, or your district? What do you care most about? How might technology help you do what you care most about even better?

A Vision for Learning

The sixteen-year-old stepdaughter of Tom Daccord arrived home from school one afternoon and started watching a movie. It was nothing too unusual. But Olivia was walking around the kitchen and pulling out cookware from the cupboards while watching it.

"What is going on?" Tom thought.

Olivia was watching a cooking show created by two students in her advanced Japanese class. She was preparing to cook the meal herself. Her teacher had challenged the students to prove that they really understood the new vocabulary. On other occasions, students might have had to write out vocabulary definitions on a worksheet or choose the correct definition on a multiple-choice quiz. But today, the teacher had provided an unstructured problem for the students to solve: how can you prove that you really understand this information? No test. No quiz. No worksheet. Their task was to create a product that communicated a persuasive understanding of the vocabulary. Since many of the terms involved things found in the kitchen, the students decided to create Iron Chef parodies and develop humorous skits, during which they used the vocabulary to teach viewers how to cook various meals.

Olivia's Japanese teacher had served up a challenging assignment for her students that inspired them to engage in real, meaningful work (and Olivia to cook a real, tasty meal for her father!). One of our fundamental commitments as educators is to prepare students for the world in which they live: to be active citizens, reflective individuals, and productive members of the working world. Yet the 21st century provides different challenges than the 20th century did. For one, the competencies required for successful work have changed significantly since 1970. Olivia's teacher was addressing those competencies in creating this assignment.

Computers and the Changing Nature of Work

Our own thinking about what skills students will need to earn a living in the working world in the decades ahead is profoundly shaped by the work of two economists: Frank Levy from MIT and Richard Murnane from Harvard's Graduate School of Education. Over the last decade, most recently in the wonderful short paper "Dancing with Robots," they have argued that computers have created fundamental shifts in the labor market (Levy & Murnane, 2014).

Computers, it turns out, are extremely good at following routines, by completing tasks that follow if-then-do patterns and solving problems with clear inputs and known end-states. Think of the very structured, predictable conversations and interactions that you might have had with an airline check-in attendant a decade ago. As we now see, that structured conversation—"Where are you going? How many bags are you checking?"—can be easily reproduced by a kiosk. Similarly, the highly routine movements that used to be undertaken by human factory workers have been replicated by robots with increasing sophistication and decreasing costs for decades.

A telling (or scary) facet of these changes is the idea that the increasing speed and power of automation means that abilities once considered "advanced" are now under threat of replacement. Consider the fact that if you used software last year to prepare your taxes, an accountant has one fewer client. Few would consider the intellectual tasks of an accountant to be "routine." Computers are also becoming more adept at understanding questions and information in context. In a high-profile defeat of two successful *Jeopardy!* champions, IBM's Watson demonstrated that computers can now analyze the meaning and context of natural human language. Factor in their ability to rapidly process huge and disparate bits of information, and it's not a stretch to say that computers are poised to replace human tasks in the economy, which would have been unthinkable only a decade ago.

Despite these challenges, entire categories of non-technology-based jobs are seeing growth. It turns out that there are still things that humans do much better than computers. In economists' terms, humans have a comparative advantage over computers in conducting tasks that require performing abstract, unstructured cognitive work that is not easily replaced by automation. Computers excel at logical tasks and following rules and statistical models. People excel at solving new problems and communicating a particular understanding of information. Technology requires prior knowledge and structure; it cannot act as an innovator in an entirely new environment. Throughout our history, the human race has adapted in the face of unforeseen and unpredictable circumstances. We innovate when faced with new challenges. We create and communicate solutions.

So over the last few decades, whereas jobs that require manual skills (like factory work) and routine cognitive tasks (like filing documents or preparing taxes) have increasingly declined, jobs that require communication, working with new information, or solving unstructured problems have increased.

In "Dancing with Robots," Levy and Murnane showcase the work of MIT economist David Autor, who investigates the changing nature of skills demands in the US labor market. In table 1.1, Autor's research shows a "hollowing out" of the labor market, which he suggests has taken place as a result of the decline of routine jobs that once provided a reasonable middle-class wage for American workers. The graph demonstrates to educators that their students will enter the most cognitively demanding labor force in US history. This is because the changes brought about by sophisticated computerization have created different and higher-skill requirements for workers. The Bureau of Labor Statistics (BLS) forecasts that the fastest-growing occupations in 2020 will involve unstructured problem solving, working with new information, and nonroutine physical activity. Students who do not develop these skills will face the real possibility of being unemployable outside of the lowest-paying jobs in the service sector.

Table 1.1: Index of Changing Work Tasks in the US Economy 1960–2009

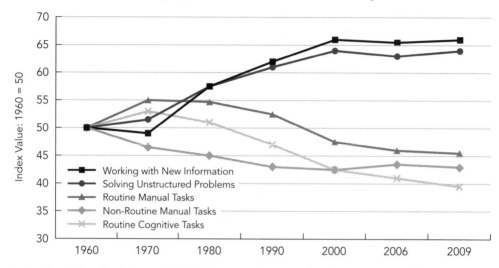

Note: Adapted from Frank Levy and Richard Murnane, "Dancing with Robots: Human Skills for Computerized Work," http://www.thirdway.org/publications/714.

Computers and the Changing Nature of Schooling

So, how do changing workplace demands relate to teaching and learning with iPads?

In our minds, schools should be leveraging iPads as "hubs of innovation" that teachers can use to nurture the types of learning skills, competencies, and habits of mind that help students develop skills for the jobs that computers cannot do. With iPads, students can research any topic that can be explored through the Internet and they can perform their understanding in a wide variety of media. These devices offer students a powerful and flexible way to solve problems and communicate their approaches to these problems. Just like in Olivia's Japanese class, students might be encouraged to create a cooking show, a public service announcement, a documentary, a video tutorial, a virtual tour, or an app. Students can research new problems and create solutions using iPads—and they can do so anytime and anyplace.

Yet in many ways our schools are still educating students to automate or outsource their learning. For example, we often assign homework questions with answers that can easily be googled. Students look up answers to our math problems, our grammar exercises, our map activities, and our lab questions on their computers without ever having to think critically at all. In short, our homework activities too often ask students to complete the rudimentary kinds of tasks that computers can be programmed to do.

The United States has a standards-based assessment education system that places great emphasis on core-knowledge acquisition and little emphasis on creative problem solving. Certainly content knowledge is important—one needs to know history to do history—but teaching today's essential skills requires an increased emphasis on deep, conceptual understanding and problem solving. Our role as educators should be to help students identify and address new opportunities and challenges—challenges that cannot be solved by applying rules. Helping students acquire and make sense of new information in problem-solving contexts, or to influence the decisions of others, should be our primary focus.

In preparing students for a world of work, we are also preparing them for an active role in a democratic society. Challenging students to solve unstructured problems by using information and tools to find creative solutions is helping students prepare for a lifetime of learning. In today's world, we communicate not only through text but also through a combination of audio, visual, and other modalities. Personal, professional, and academic forms of communication are increasingly being produced in these varied forms, featuring elements such as online video and audio, interactive charts, graphs, maps, polls, and surveys. These forms of communication are also increasingly found on a diverse span of platforms: a webpage, a text message, an IM chat, a social network, and more. Having critical-inquiry skills related to various communication forms and platforms is now part of the primer for 21st century literacy. Literacy skills developed in mobile, online environments are crucial for this millennium's student and foundational to the development of effective global citizens in today's networked world.

We should point out that Olivia and her classmates took ownership over the information in their assignment. They decided how they were going to convey their particular understanding of the content. It was their product, and not surprisingly, they were fully engaged with conveying it. (Now in her twenties, Olivia says the cooking activity was the most memorable lesson she experienced and still recalls the vocabulary she learned as part of it.) It was also a collaborative and interdependent effort: students worked together and learned from one another, and Olivia had to watch her classmates' video to learn how to cook the meal. It was not just up to the teacher to "cover" all the material or to "teach" the students all the content; instead, learning was a shared responsibility. Lifelong learners understand that passion for learning comes from pursuing one's interests and that learning is not an isolated activity but rather is enriched by shared contributions of others.

As we face the most demanding labor market and civic sphere in human history, and a time of rapid change in patterns of human creation, there is much that can be done to prepare students that does not involve technology. The heart of great classrooms has always been caring, passionate adults asking compelling questions that motivate students to deeply understand important skills and ideas. But it is also increasingly difficult to prepare young people for a digital world without letting them rehearse in mobile, online spaces. We agree with Levy and Murnane's theory in "Dancing with Robots" that learning to work with new information is essential and that it is impossible to think about learning to work with diverse sources of information without first learning how to efficiently navigate the Internet. The end product of solving complex problems is often a performance—some of those performances are still written documents or mathematical computations, but increasingly students need to be able to perform their understanding in print and in person with media and online. Even those students who are excited about doing work in the trades need to be prepared to sell their services in an online marketplace, to constantly update their skills in online learning settings, and to participate in a civic sphere conducted in a networked world.

Putting technology in the service of learning, in our view, means putting technology in the service of preparing students to solve unstructured problems and communicate persuasively with deep understanding. That's our vision of what great schools do. We want to share that vision here, in the introduction to this book, so that you understand how our vision shapes the chapters that follow. You should understand that our goal here is not about how to click buttons on apps; it's about how to transform schools and change kids' lives.

Your own vision for teaching may be different. Whatever it is, it should be particular to the culture and the needs of the children that you serve in your particular community. Sometimes to help teachers think about these issues in a fun way, we'll ask the questions: What does awesome look like? If you are doing your best possible work, better than you have ever done before, what do the learners look like on the other end? However you define your vision for powerful learning in your own classroom, school, or district, we hope that you will reflect on it and refine it throughout this book, even as we get into the details of workflow, app selection, and specific teaching techniques.

The Journey Ahead

As we approach the challenge of creating powerful learning environments with iPads, we use five bedrock principles to keep us grounded. These principles shape our teaching, our professional development work, and the book you have in your hands.

Here are the five principles:

1. *Technology must be in the service of learning.* Without a clear vision for learning, technology is the engine of a ship without a compass.

2. *Tablets are not computers.* There are some things tablets do much better than computers; there are some things they do much worse. Focus on exploiting what they do best.

3. *iPads are mobile, flexible media-production devices, not repositories of apps.* Students and teachers do not need lists of dozens of apps. Instead, they need a shared vision of powerful, student-owned learning, and a small list of flexible apps for creation and curation.

4. *The iPad has a design bias toward content consumption; great teaching has a design bias toward student production.* To make the iPad support powerful learning, we need to work with educators on moving from having students consume content with it to having them curate and create content.

5. *Technology initiatives will only work if we can gain broad support from community stakeholders.* These stakeholders include parents, teachers, students, and the community.

In the first chapter of this book, we develop these key principles. We share stories of some of the most successful school-wide and district-wide tablet initiatives that we know about, and we will show how they demonstrate these principles. By the time you are done with the first chapter, we hope that you will have a sense of the ideals behind the efforts to improve teaching and learning by incorporating iPads.

Chapters 2 and 3 of this book contain the heart of our ideas about the iPad classroom. These chapters focus on three Cs: consumption, curation, and creation (by federal statute, every EdTech book needs to have a cluster of at least three Cs). In this part of the book, we get into the nitty-gritty of creating meaningful teaching and learning environments that incorporate iPads. For many classroom teachers, chapters 2 and 3 will be the heart of the book.

In chapter 4, we pan back out and look at systemically building technological capacity. We save our favorite part—teacher professional learning—for last. In our concluding chapter, we share everything that we have learned about teaching technology to educators, from our overall approach to hands-on challenges we have encountered in our workshops with teachers, which will allow you to take what you have learned and use it to build a professional learning program for iPad integration in your own school. We also explain how we design our workshops, so that, as much as possible, you can create learning environments for teachers that model the principles we value.

The only way your school's investment in tablet devices will have a real return is if your school invests just as much in teachers as it invests in technology.

That's the plan. So, grab your iPad and play along. And remember to keep asking yourself, What does "awesome" look like? Now, let's get to work.

Consuming Content on the iPad: Diverse Pathways for Diverse Learners

In the apocryphal photo of the iPad launch, the tablet rests in the lap of Steve Jobs, as he reclines in a leather chair on the stage of the iPad release ceremony. The iPad is a device that was made for reading and watching, for sitting back, for consuming media. While we certainly want our students to read for pleasure, we certainly don't want to craft learning environments modeled on a figure who sits in a reclining posture.

Teaching and learning involve the consumption of media, sometimes from a leisurely posture where a love of media can be nurtured and sometimes from an active posture with a forward lean, sharp eyes, and readiness to pounce and engage a piece of text or frame of video. That said, far too much of our classroom time is spent delivering content and not nearly enough of it is spent empowering students to be producers and publishers. So while we will start our journey into iPad integration by looking at using tablets for collecting ideas, we hope that no one gets stuck at this stage.

One of the signature challenges presented by the surge of interest in iPads is helping educators look beyond the simplest use of iPads in classrooms and to experiment with the most transformative. Instead of using iPads as a library of books or a Rolodex of apps, teachers should imagine the possibilities of an iPad as a flexible, mobile platform for creating multimedia performances of understanding.

One framework that educators often find helpful in thinking about technology-mediated learning environments is the collect-relate-create-donate (CRCD) framework proposed by human-computer-interaction expert Ben Shneiderman (2003) in his book *Leonardo's Laptop*. Shneiderman suggests that rich technology projects be designed along a pattern. Students start by collecting information, either from their own research or from teacher-curated readings, lectures, and materials, and then collaboratively work in teams to create a performance of their understanding. This can be a paper, poster, presentation, play, diorama, computer program, website, or anything else that allows them to make their learning public. Students then share their work with a larger audience by presenting it to a specific group or publishing it on the web. This chapter offers some ideas for the collecting phase, in the hope that this kind of learning is a launching point for creating performances of understanding.

Universal Access

Assistive Technology Specialist Karen Janowski bought an iPad the first week it launched. As she explained it: "I saw the potential the minute it came out. I said to myself, I have to get one because this is going to be a game changer for the struggling learners with whom I work."

Since purchasing that first device, she has motivated her school to purchase them for the students and seen the multiple ways the iPad benefits them, specifically in the areas of organization, repetition and review, visual support, communication, and reading to make their learning public.

One of Janowski's students is a fourth grader who has cerebral palsy in addition to a learning disability and visual tracking issues, so not only is holding a book and turning pages difficult for him but so is comprehending and following fourth-grade-level book text. The teacher, along with the school district, gave this student an iPad and purchased Voice Dream Reader (an app Janowski lauds as "phenomenal"), which brings in text from places like Google Drive, Bookshare, and other locations on the web, and allows students to listen to it read aloud with a customized a visual presentation. Within a week, Janowski explained, "his mother said he was reading the books his friends were reading that, up until that time, he was unable to do . . . . Now he was devouring books."

In another case, Janowski pointed to a ninth-grade student who, despite "intensive remediation," still struggled with reading, decoding, and fluency. He took to Audiobooks.com, a free app that offers high-quality human narration of classic books in the public domain. "We gave [the iPad] to him on Friday, and when I saw him on the following Friday he had almost completed *The Invisible Man* by H. G. Wells, a book he would never, ever have been able to tackle independently," Janowski said.

"Now, students are able to read the curriculum and content independently," Janowski said. "In the past, they may have had to depend on another adult or a parent at home. I'm passionate about this [the iPad] because it makes such a huge difference for kids."

Among the first groups eager to explore new possibilities of the iPad have been educators working with populations on the margins: special educators, teachers of English language learners, reading specialists, and their kindred colleagues. The iPad offers new hope for these students who have been poorly served by the shape of our traditional curriculum to bypass some long-standing obstacles to learning. Fortunately, every time special educators develop new strategies for working with populations on the margin, we find that they are additionally building best practices for supporting all learners. So, a fundamental goal of this chapter is to introduce strategies for consuming content on the iPad that can help all learners.

One of the signature findings of the cognitive revolution that has taken place in mind, brain, and education research over the last few decades has been the overwhelming recognition of the diversity of human brains. In our population of students, there is a stunning variety of talents and capacities, and any given peculiarity can be both a great strength and a great weakness. For instance, an incredibly high proportion of the world's leading astrophysicists are dyslexic. As it turns out, in the complex architecture of the brain-eye connection, some of us have very strong central vision and others have very strong peripheral vision. Those with strong peripheral vision often have trouble with dyslexia and are distracted by words appearing to be scattered all over a page. However, their strong peripheral vision is a critical asset in finding patterns in wavelength images, which happens to be the core competency of many astrophysicists.

We also now know that information that is absorbed through multiple sensory modalities or pathways addresses a wider range of learners and increases both comprehension and use. For instance, the retention of text is often improved when words and pictures are received rather than words alone. We also know that students process information differently when they are reading than when they are doing other types of processes such as mathematical calculations. In all, our students have processing differences that influence how they will handle information through text, visual, aural, or kinesthetic pathways (Darling-Hammond, Rosso, Austin, Orcutt, & Martin, 2015).

Despite the great diversity in our capacities, our curriculum materials are often narrowly constructed, with a focus on text. Some advocates have gone so far as to call the curriculum "print disabled"—meaning that it does not support the learning of people who struggle with decoding print. Note the important shift here: it is not the kid who is disabled; it is the published materials that are disabled and incapable of doing their job of supporting learning.

In response to the severe disabilities of our print curriculum, many researchers and educators have embraced a set of principles called universal design for learning (UDL), which calls into consideration three important aspects of learning:

- Students should have access to curriculum content through diverse forms of media.

- Students should demonstrate their understanding through diverse forms of media.

- Students should have multiple pathways through which they become engaged and motivated to learn.

Students still struggling to decode text should not be prevented from learning science content because of their challenges in reading; they should be able to get the content through video, audio, and other strategies even as they continue to develop their reading skills.

There is a great deal of exciting research happening that is exploring how we can use emerging technologies to transform our curriculum materials and make them more accessible to students. For instance, a recent study by researchers at the Harvard-Smithsonian Astrophysics Observatory designed an e-reader that limited students to viewing only three to four giant words on a screen at a time, with a simple mechanism that allowed them to scroll rapidly through the words. For some readers with dyslexia that stems from visual difficulties, their reading fluency, speed, and comprehension increased substantially as a result of using this device. Through this kind of research, educators and publishers are developing more ways for technology to help all students access the content of the curriculum.

In an ideal world, all the resources that we use in our schools would have this UDL support built right into them to remedy the print disabilities in our textbooks and supplements. Unfortunately, we have not reached that point yet, so the classroom champions of our struggling learners have been teaching students how to enhance their materials using iPads and creating this accessibility for themselves.

Core Accessibility Features

A simple step toward enabling greater access to content is utilizing iPad Accessibility features. Accessibility, located under Settings on the iPad, provides access to various features to meet the needs of those with learning differences or delayed development of motor skills. One such feature is Speak Selection. Speak Selection is especially useful for language development as it enables the iPad to read text from webpages and certain apps, as well as e-books and iMessages.

Visit http://edtechteacher.org/tutorials/accessibility for an EdTechTeacher video tutorial on how to use the Speak Selection features in the iPad's Accessibility folder. (All links for this book are also at www.learningsciences.com/bookresources and edtechteacher.org/ipadbooklinks.)

When you double-tap text to highlight it and then tap Speak in any of the iPad's applications, the selected text is read aloud. The speaking rate can also be adjusted to suit an individual student's needs. You can even choose a particular dialect. Speak Selection also works with foreign languages. So, for instance, it will read text from a web article in Spanish if you instruct it to. Students can also have words highlighted as they are reading to help them follow along. For young students just learning to read and write and students with learning differences (such as dyslexia) as well as for those learning a new language, Speak Selection is invaluable.

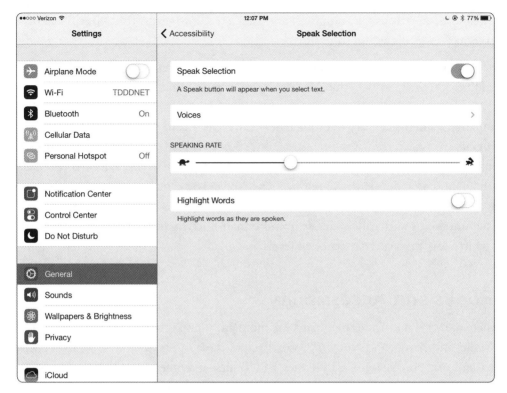

Figure 1.1: The iPad's Speak Selection screen is located in the Accessibility folder.

Another crucial part of UDL is the provision of support for readers right inside their curriculum materials. As far as traditionally static texts like dictionaries, encyclopedias, and thesauri, the iPad has the ability to leverage these resources more flexibly than a hardbound book. Whereas, at one time, you had to consult separate volumes for dictionaries and thesauri, now a tap of a button will bring up the equivalent information. Dictionaries are also embedded within various reading apps and web browsers, removing a significant barrier to fluency. Readers can define words with a simple double-tap of the screen. This is especially helpful when working with science articles, works of literature, and primary historical sources in which students are likely to encounter unfamiliar terms.

When students find unknown words, they can double-tap the word, select Define, and the definition will come up; they can even make notes or rewrite the sentence within the text by paraphrasing the definition in the new version. Hyperlinks to antonyms, synonyms, and example sentences can now be augmented by audio recordings of the words and context.

These features help the iPad speak to students, but students can speak to the iPad as well. With Dictation, students can take notes, search the web, write a report, and answer email, simply by using their voice. When you tap the Microphone button,

Dictation converts words, numbers, and characters into text. (Tom loves Dictation for notes on readings and to-do lists.)

Apple's built-in personal assistant, Siri, can also help students by providing reminders like "English paper is due Monday" and scheduling activities and events. Siri is also integrated with VoiceOver—an advanced screen reader—so that visually impaired students can ask questions, hear the answer read out loud, and otherwise interact with the screen. Whereas Speak Selection only reads selected text, VoiceOver enables visually impaired students to touch an object on the screen to have it read out loud; it also provides alerts and notifications. VoiceOver can also speak each character as a student types and entire words when the student enters a space or punctuation. The function is currently available in more than thirty languages, making it a great resource for language learners of all levels.

iBooks and Accessibility

There are several e-reader platforms for the iPad, such as Apple's iBooks, Amazon's Kindle, and Barnes and Nobles's Nook. Each of these can be used to download both free and paid books as well as PDF files, EPUB files, and other documents for the web.

Each of these popular e-reading platforms has its own set of built-in Accessibility features. For instance, in iBooks, one option is to change the font size, as shown in figure 1.2. Reducing text size allows more of the text to be displayed on the page at once, which can be especially helpful when a student is attempting to consume a single passage. For students with vision impairments or those who want to make it easier to see a sentence or passage, increasing the font size provides flexibility, which is not possible with printed books. Another option that iBooks offers is the ability to change the background color of the screen, also shown in the figure. Looking at screens for too long causes eye fatigue, so changing the background color to black or sepia can provide a more relaxing experience. In addition, for situations in which students are viewing the screen in a low-light setting, like watching a film clip in class, reversing the font and background colors allows them to read without disturbing others.

The iPad's backlight can also be made lighter or darker to make reading at night or in the sun more comfortable. Additionally, the iBooks app formats the screen both horizontally and vertically, depending on how students prefer to hold the iPad. Beyond simple comfort, changing the orientation determines how much text students see at once, accommodating their pace and the layout of the text.

As emerging research from the Harvard-Smithsonian Lab suggests, more of these kinds of accessibility features are on their way. The first students to take advantage of these opportunities are those with diagnosed learning disabilities. These various features are overcoming the print disabilities of our curriculum and opening new

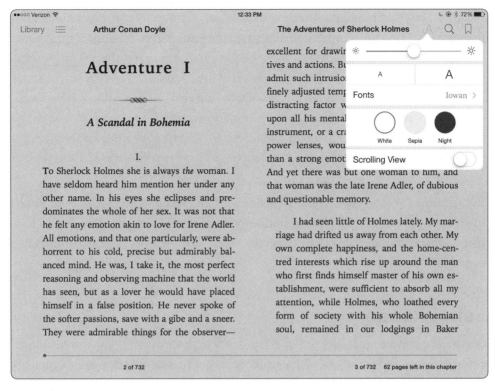

Figure 1.2: When reading *The Adventures of Sherlock Holmes* in iBooks, you have the option to change the font size and change the background color.

pathways for learning for students with special needs. At the same time, these features have the potential to benefit all learners by making reading more comfortable, supporting endurance for longer reading sessions, and providing in-text scaffolds to understand difficult words or passages. Over time, many readers will make a habit of customizing their reading platform to suit their own needs, the text, and the situation.

A Multimedia Curriculum

It may seem simple, but one of the first things that we do in our iPad classroom workshops is remind people that every tablet has a web browser. For a variety of reasons, apps dominate the discussion around iPads, which is somewhat unfortunate. Sure, there is a boatload of educational apps, but while a few are good, most are wanting. The most extraordinary learning resource ever created, however, is the World Wide Web—and portable, instant-on/instant-off access to the Internet is one of the signature benefits of using tablets in the classroom. Tablets with Internet connections also allow teachers to use much more than printouts and textbooks and access diverse sets of resources in their curriculum.

Consuming traditional publications in a digital environment involves much more than a simple substitution for pen and paper. For one thing, it speaks to the power of access. National newspapers such as the *New York Times* and the *Washington Post* have their own webpages and apps, as do many international news agencies like the *London Times* and *Al Jazeera*. These can enable a diversity of educational experiences, such as a social studies class comparing and contrasting front pages of newspapers from around the country on a particular day to compare different perspectives, or a history class that wants to dig into the archives to study headlines on a historical date.

In addition to current events and newspaper archives, students can access records and databases, putting primary sources like the Congressional Record at their fingertips. Having previously difficult-to-find texts available in a few taps provides students with primary sources, a broader perspective, and—with teacher guidance—increased digital and cultural understanding.

Safari Reader

Reader is a simple and nifty Safari feature that strips away the kind of unwanted advertisements and peripheral elements of webpages such as that shown in figure 1.3.

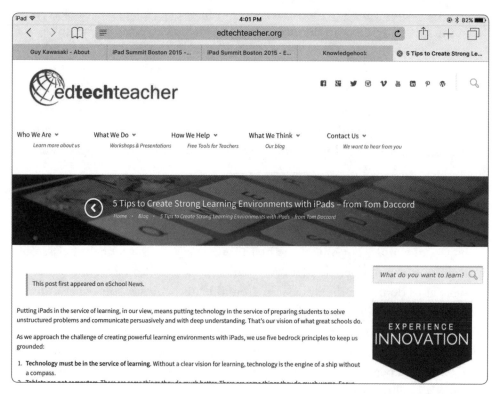

Figure 1.3: The advertisements and peripheral elements surrounding an article like this one can be stripped away with Safari Reader.

The Reader icon is made up of four small parallel lines that sit to the far left of the URL bar on the top of the screen, as shown in figure 1.4. To activate it, you simply tap the Reader icon.

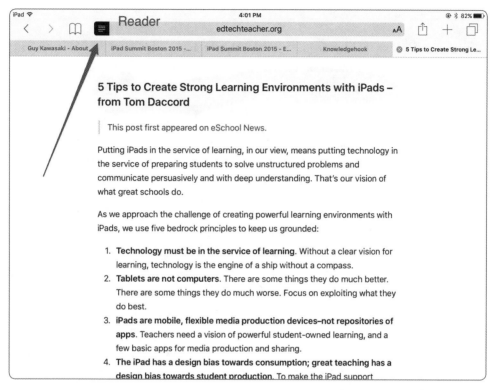

Figure 1.4: If you tap the Reader icon, the peripheral elements will be removed and you'll see only the article and associated image.

The caveat is that Reader does not appear on all webpages. It only appears in single-page articles and posts, typically found in online newspapers, magazines, and blogs. Moving beyond giving you access to texts, the iPad provides many multimedia options. For example, here are some ways that researching historical figures can go beyond simply reading a book, a collection of primary sources, or an academic journal when using the tablet:

- *Thomas Jefferson*: You can read The Writings of Thomas Jefferson in iBooks or listen to *The Thomas Jefferson Hour* podcast during which Mr. Jefferson comments on current events.

- *William Shakespeare*: You can listen to lectures by professors at Oxford, Cambridge, and Stanford via iTunes U or use the Shakespeare Pro app to examine the First Folios and Quartos.

- *Rosalind Franklin*: There are a variety of videos on YouTube that you can watch about her story, articles on her life that you can read in *Scientific American* or *Nova*, and videos you can watch of interviews with her biographer or commentary from other scientists about the impact of her contributions.

Using an iPad for these multiple modes of research and exploration allows students to access sophisticated multimedia resources. It would take a teacher an incredible amount of time to find and provide the equivalent resources for students, and the cost can often be prohibitive. By leveraging the access that an iPad provides, teachers can focus on the development of students' skills rather than spending their time collecting and photocopying articles. Meanwhile, students can access materials in ways that support their individual learning rather than relying on whole-class instruction about a single text.

Previously, repositories of expert knowledge were limited by their physical size and distribution of resources and forced students to all work at the same level. For example, your class might have been reading a book written by an expert on a specific topic, but you might not have enough copies of it to provide to the entire class. With an iPad, however, students can each access these resources on their personal iPad at their own time and pace. Consider subject-specific resources like field guides, where it would be impractical for every student to have their own physical copy for a short unit. Free apps such as Leafsnap give students high-resolution pictures of plant leaves that they can sort by first, last, or scientific name, as well as tap to see where else in the country that particular leaf can be found. Students can also take their own pictures of leaves in the playground or their backyards to compare to the database. This allows students to personalize a lesson to their individual environments.

While audiobooks have existed for a long time in analog format (i.e., records, tapes, CDs), audio as a medium of content now spreads across podcasts, lectures, poetry readings, author excerpts, and even oral histories. iTunes U offers a catalog of lectures and even full courses from top-tier universities and colleges complete with audio lectures. Students studying psychology, for example, can download clips on adolescent psychology and connect it to their own lives. With the NPR app, students can make a playlist of news stories on national and international events that have a connection to their local news. Tucking an iPad into their bag and plugging in headphones makes the auditory learning process even more accessible, in that students can listen along to books downloaded from LibriVox, or added to Audiobooks, as well as to podcasts from iTunes.

Inkling and 3D Books

Increasingly, publishers are finding new ways of incorporating engaging accessibility features into rich multimedia resources. Inkling is a publisher producing interactive digital books with a variety of kinesthetic and interactive innovations: 3D simulations, interactive maps and photos, embedded videos, audio commentaries, music, formative quizzes, the ability to share notes and bookmarks, and more. Figure 1.5 shows a page from an Inkling science textbook with an Add a Note option.

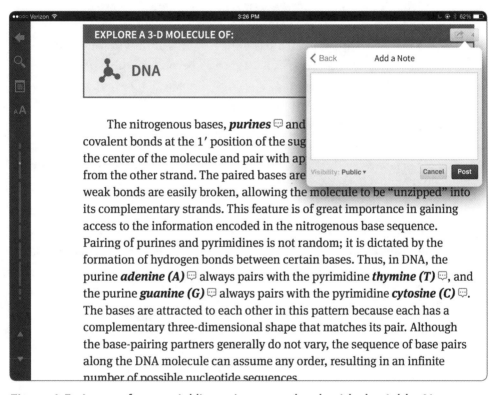

Figure 1.5: A page from an Inkling science textbook with the Add a Note option open.

A tour of a free Inkling chapter via https://support.inkling.com/hc/en-us/articles /202480653-Get-a-free-chapter allows you to take stock of the books' immersive features. For starters, books feature a scrolling interface along with elements such as vocabulary definitions that pop up on the page when touched. Inkling images also contain hot spots that, when touched, allow users to explore deep into an object. For example, a user can go from viewing an entire bed of flowers to viewing the minute depiction of a single petal's cell photosynthesis. Chapters also contain video presentations of content being discussed on the pages.

Another interesting feature is the ability to go to a specific point in a piece of music (say a Mozart piece) while the user is listening to it in an Inkling textbook. Inkling books also include audio recordings by experts on related chapter topics as well as formative assessment tools such as interactive quizzes that give the user the ability to score their own results. The benefit of an iPad is that all of these activities are performed and assessed on a single device, instead of relying on multiple tools, activities, and handouts. But, arguably, the most impressive elements are the 3D components. These are objects that can be rotated, zoomed in and out on, and otherwise manipulated on an iPad. In Inkling's *Microbiology: A Systems Approach* (Cowan, 2011), students can conduct a virtual tour of chromosomes where they are able to rotate and zoom in and out on them, as shown in figure 1.6. This affords an opportunity for hands-on, exploratory learning of cell structure well beyond anything possible in 2D. Indeed, many biology teachers attempt in vain to simulate a 3D exploration of molecules by offering wooden or plastic models to their students. With Inkling, students can explore and manipulate chromosomes in ways that could never be accomplished in 2D paper or wooden structures. It took only a minute spent exploring chromosomes in 3D before we wished that we had more than static 2D pictures in our own high school biology textbooks.

Visit https://edtechteacher.org/tutorials/inkling for an EdTechTeacher video tutorial demonstrating Inkling's immersive features. (All links for this book are also at www.learningsciences.com/bookresources and edtechteacher.org/ipadbooklinks.)

So, what does the new world of kinesthetic learning on iPads look like now that students can touch and tour 3D elements and immerse themselves in various interactive elements? The text, simulations, and video can be combined in powerful ways to help students understand content knowledge. In physics class, interspacing a narrative explanation of pulley systems with an interactive pulley simulation and accompanying video promotes the integration of visual and textual learners. In art class, analyzing brushstrokes in paintings by zooming in on artistic elements and reading about an artist's other work provides a richer experience than simply relying on a basic explanation. In an elementary classroom, a 3D tour of a building's architectural elements can help children formulate an abstract understanding of volume and spatial relationships. The juxtaposition of text with kinesthetic interactions and other interactive elements allows for a deeper exploration of content.

Inkling is only one example of a publisher and app developer offering a more immersive, flexible, and robust consumption experience than we have ever seen before. Ben Shneiderman's CRCD framework, the process by which students are collecting information from either their own research or teacher-curated materials, is also being transformed on the iPad in substantial ways. Interactive platforms, diverse multimedia, constantly updated and searchable content, and various media

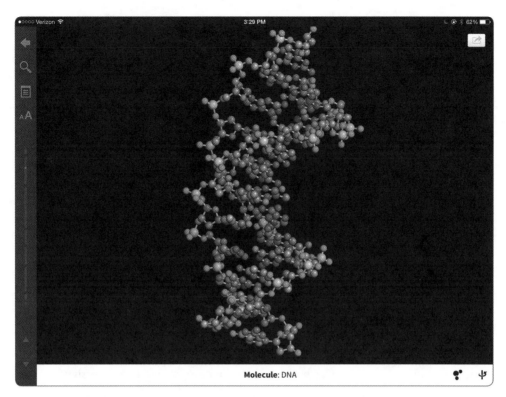

Figure 1.6: A page in Inkling's microbiology textbook with the 3D, interactive chromosome simulation zoomed in on.

for consuming content are being combined with traditional platforms to alter the collection process while facilitating exploration and personalization.

Focused Versus Connected Consumption: Debating the Future of Reading

All of these diverse kinds of interactive texts raise another set of questions for educators: Do the new forms of media enabled by emerging technologies signal a shift to new modes of reading? Now that we have access not just to books but also to articles, blog posts, Tumblrs, tweets, images, videos, Vines, and more, to what extent is the act of reading substantially changing? To what extent do educators need to rethink what it means to teach students to read?

To oversimplify the inquiry, we might say that there are now two modes of reading: focused and connected.

Focused reading is the mode of reading that we have been teaching in schools for decades, where we ask young people to deeply engage with a single text. In the words of Mark Ott, the chair of the English Department at Deerfield Academy, "Students used to sit at a desk with nothing but a copy of Thoreau's *Walden* and experience sustained engagement with Thoreau's ideas. We want to preserve that experience in a world where devices are constantly competing for their attention." Whether the copy of *Walden* is the $4.99 paperback edition or the free digital copy from the iBooks library, educators still believe in the importance of being able to read a single text without distraction for an extended period of time.

By contrast, the connected mode of reading celebrates and takes advantage of the diversity of reading resources made possible in a networked world. In the connected reading mode, we ask students to treat texts as nodes in a network of information. Connected readers recognize that weaving together multiple texts is often essential to understanding a topic from different perspectives. When doing research, connected reading draws on the ability to synthesize key ideas across multiple articles, book chapters, and websites. University of South California researcher Henry Jenkins (2009) suggests that following a contemporary media narrative requires a skill set that he calls "transmedia navigation," which describes the ability to follow a story across Twitter hashtags, newspaper articles, live streams of police scanners, blog posts, and other forms of media.

In the past, schools have sometimes made a strong distinction between reading as a solitary activity that is done at home and discussing texts as a social activity that is done at school. Increasingly, social technologies break down these barriers, allowing the act of reading to take place in communal settings, leveraging social technologies to allow users to share notes, highlighted passages, questions, and ideas. In an extreme application of this connected reading, Diana Kimball, a fellow at the Berkman Center for Internet & Society at Harvard University, has formed a "24-hour book club" where groups sign up to read the same book in a twenty-four-hour period, using Twitter to share reactions, favorite passages, questions, hunches, and insights.

Although the focused and connected modes of reading are both vital, they require different habits, disciplines, and settings, and they serve different ends. To oversimplify, focused reading on tablets requires cultivating self-control; connected reading on tablets requires developing new skills and practices.

To be sure, encouraging students to read a book on a device loaded with games, social tools, and notifications constantly clamoring for their attention is a dangerous game. On the one hand, given all of these distractions, the plain print book seems like the perfect platform for sustained engagement. At the same time, in the decades ahead, many students will read on devices that—as we have pointed out—have features that are integral in enhancing the reading experience. In addition, cultivating the discipline to maintain their concentration on the most useful elements while engaging with a potentially distracting platform can be a powerful life lesson for students.

Howard Rheingold (2012), in his fine book *Net Smart*, praises the art of attention as the habit of keeping at the front of one's mind the purpose of using an online environment. If students' purpose is focused reading, then they need to learn to recognize that every move they make away from the text and into another online space is a distraction from sustained engagement. If the purpose is connected reading, students need to recognize how to strike the right balance between exploring a network of hyperlinked texts and not wandering away from the core purpose of their reading. The first step in helping students develop these skills is to teach them to recognize attention as a skill that requires them to metacognitively reflect on their attention strategies and weaknesses and how to best exercise their own attention muscles. Students can learn to create a digital environment conducive to attention and concentration. For iPads, iOS 7 has a Guided Access feature designed to limit user activity to a particular app or webpage. Somewhat hidden under the Accessibility menu in the General Settings, Guided Access allows users to lock themselves in to a particular app, disable all notifications, and require a passcode to log out, as shown in figure 1.7. It can also be programmed to lock users into certain areas of a webpage, not just the page itself. Although doing these things will not disable distraction, it can set it a few more taps away. Yes, teachers also have the option of setting the passcode on their students' iPad themselves and locking the student into a particular place, but it is a time-consuming task and developing student awareness of their own tendencies toward distraction is a much better long-term strategy for developing attention skills.

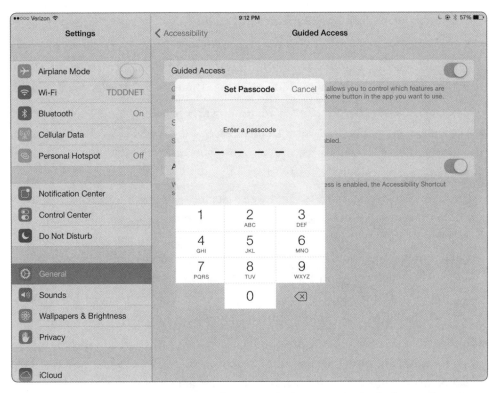

Figure 1.7: Users can set a passcode in Guided Access to lock themselves in to an app, or even a webpage.

Visit http://edtechteacher.org/tutorials/guidedaccess for an EdTechTeacher video tutorial on using Guided Access features.

Actually, shutting down all apps before reading can be a kind of ritual of concentration, like clearing way books and papers from one's desk before sitting down to read. It also makes it slightly more difficult to jump into a game that needs to load or a web browser preloaded with interesting pages. Such are the 21st century methods of creating a clear desk for reading.

In terms of connected modes of reading, there are new apps emerging that attempt to network people and texts into social reading environments. Subtext is an innovative social reading app that allows teachers to select a text, distribute it to students, and then place students into reading groups. In essence, the app allows students and teachers to read books collaboratively while sharing comments and information. In these groups, students can share notes, highlight passages, ask questions, engage in discussions, and respond to teacher prompts.

While reading, participants can insert text, emoticons, questions, links, and thoughts into the margins of the book, as shown in figure 1.8. When other readers jump into the text, they can see the notations and reply to the existing thoughts in a discussion thread that is neatly tucked away in the margins of the text. Reading becomes a shared, communal act that is no longer limited to classroom discussion but also takes place during the experience of reading.

Teachers can pose questions, poll students, insert media in the margins, and track student progress throughout a book. In this way, a teacher can layer in resources and activities while opening up new avenues to engage students and develop reading skills.

Subtext enables teachers to personalize reading experiences beyond what is possible with standard annotation tools, as it facilitates access to Google Docs, Google Search, and Google Drive. To see its features at work, you can watch Subtext in action at http://vimeo.com/readwithsubtext/videos.

There are also several new apps and web platforms supporting increased collaboration in the research process. Zotero is a website run by the Center for History and New Media at George Mason University that is designed to support collaborative research. Zotero's web interface works great on tablets, and the tool helps both groups and individual students to organize diverse sources for research projects and manage bibliographic information. Students can upload resources to a shared library, construct a single shared bibliography, and share notes on sources.

In the CRCD framework, the process of collecting information also includes annotating information. In the next section on active reading, we discuss tools that help students to annotate texts and organize their notes and annotations in order to find the connections across different sources and learning experiences. Students can use

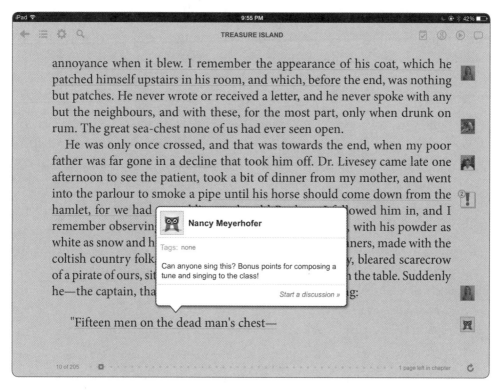

Figure 1.8: A Subtext program screen where students can tap on the icons in the margin to reveal comments, resources, or discussions created by other students and the teacher.

these kinds of tools and active-reading approaches to manage the incredible diversity of resources and types of text and media that are now available to them.

While digital tools can shape our cognitive experiences in undesirable ways, many of the personal drawbacks of technology can be avoided. We simply need to develop new habits to make the most of our new tools. If our tools can distract us, then we need to learn more about focusing our attention and managing distraction. Used wisely, we can choose to read *Walden* alone in quiet repose, or we can choose to read *Walden* in a community with peers and mentors, where students divided by geography read together, as the Transcendentalists might have done in Emerson's manse. Without these deliberate efforts to rethink reading, we may find, as Thoreau said of the emerging technology of his own time, "We do not ride on the railroad; it rides upon us."

Active Reading

As educators, we often want students to be actively engaged in making meaning of their reading. This is true whether they're drilling down into a single text or reading across a variety of sources; whether they're reading on a default screen or with highly personalized settings; or whether they're reading a plain-text document or a multimedia resource. Certainly we sometimes want to see our students flopped back in a beanbag chair just taking in the pleasures of a great book, but we also want to cultivate students' ability to be active readers, mining texts for meaning and understanding.

Over the years, educators have developed a suite of strategies to help students take an active reading stance when working with print materials: we teach students to highlight, to make marginalia, to create notes in various structures, and so forth. There are now a variety of apps and features that allow students to conduct all of these good practices on a tablet, and new practices are emerging that take advantage of the affordances of the iPad.

If you were to ask students at Burlington High School—the first school in the United States to develop a one-to-one iPad program—about how tablets have changed their daily lives in school, many of them would start talking about how they use Evernote. Evernote is a note-taking and annotation app that many students use to replace and surpass a stack of notebooks and three-ring binders for every class.

Evernote allows students to first upload documents and webpages into the program and then actively engage these documents as they are reading. Students can type comments in the margins, highlight the text with different colors (red for important quotes, green for vocabulary words, blue for general notes, etc.), handwrite notes or comments, and even insert audio notes and mind maps to summarize complex ideas. So most active reading strategies that a student might be able to do with a printed document can be done inside the program.

Notes can also be in the form of blank documents, allowing students to take more extensive notes on books or movies that cannot be uploaded into a single note. Again, students can type, write, add pictures, and add audio on these documents. Students can also take notes on class lectures or discussions and add a photograph of the black- or whiteboard at the end of the period to document the day's activity. Teachers who use graphic organizers to help students learn different note-taking and annotation strategies can distribute these organizers as PDF documents, and these can then be uploaded to Evernote and edited or completed by students. When there are activities that would be best written down with pen and paper—like complicated science lab notes—they can be recorded by hand and then photographed and uploaded into a new Evernote note.

Each of these notes can then be organized inside a folder to create a comprehensive record of a student's activity and learning in one class—with the annotated readings, reading notes, class notes, and teacher documents (like syllabi and worksheets) all organized in a single folder. Many students at Burlington High School will tell you that they create one Evernote folder for each class, so that their entire high school note-taking system is embedded into a single application. Evernote also has the added benefit of allowing students to sync notes across every device they own—their phone, tablet, laptop, desktop computer, and so on—so that they can take notes on a tablet in class and then use those notes to write a paper on their laptop.

Visit http://edtechteacher.org/evernote/ for an EdTechTeacher video tutorial on using Evernote on the iPad.

Of course, there are other apps that perform these and similar functions as well. Notability is another annotation app that has a nice interface for annotating documents. Explain Everything is a screencasting app, which we will discuss in chapter 3, where students can upload documents and make a recording of their active reading. All of the e-reader platforms have some of these annotation tools built into them. By the time this book is published, there is no doubt that there will be other new apps designed to support this kind of active reading. The key idea is that there are a variety of ways to extend the existing active-reading practices from pen and paper to tablets, and there are myriad new possibilities that tablets offer to enhance the ways that students engage with texts.

Evernote Use at Montclair Kimberley Academy

Montclair Kimberley Academy, a large preK–12 independent day school in New Jersey, uses Evernote extensively to collect and organize student work created on iPads. Each iPad is set up with a generic email account for sending messages (e.g., schooliPads@school.edu). In addition, each iPad has its Contacts app populated with every teacher's "Email Directly to Evernote" email address. This allows a student to send content directly to a teacher's Evernote account from any iPad using any app that has an email export function.

As teachers collect more and more content, they need to develop ways to organize student work. One way they are doing this is to teach students in second and third grades how to include the target notebook name (by using the @ symbol) and tags (by using the # symbol) in the subject line of the email to leverage Evernote's Notebook and Tagging systems. Evernote automatically dates each note, so that teachers do not have to worry about keeping track of them. They can then easily sort through their students' notebooks to trace their progress. For instance, one second- and third-grade teacher organizes her students' video artifacts in her Evernote notebook by student so that she is able to see each child's development in applying the reading strategy in an individual notebook.

Recently, the primary school music director has been using Evernote Shared Notebooks to curate content for each class. She described the progress enabled by Evernote in terms of updating versions of songs and lyrics recorded by her classes. Previously, she had been burning CDs and/or emailing lyrics and song files to teachers and then asking them to share the materials with students. Now, she simply creates a shared Evernote Notebook for each class, and in each note, she adds the music file and song lyrics so that teachers can easily share the materials with the class. This allows teachers and students to know that they always have the updated versions of the music and lyrics. This content curation has not only been helpful for the music director's intended audiences of students and teachers; it has also been helpful for her own organization as she manages the complexity of leading five different grade levels through their music curricula.

Here is Reshan Richards, director of education technology, on how Evernote is used by teachers and students at Montclair Academy to address higher-order learning processes:

> While empowering our students with iPads and other mobile devices unlocks tremendous potential to create, communicate, and collaborate, the still unanswered question is how do we determine that they have also gained greater understanding, reflected on their learning, and mastered content? Can these same devices support our students as they engage in those higher order processes? Will curating all of this content into a portfolio or some other structure support this quest for higher understanding and allow students to connect with their own learning?
>
> Evernote provides one possible solution to the challenge. The ability to sync across multiple devices, to email directly to a notebook, to include photos and audio recordings in notes, and to share notes, makes Evernote a powerful assessment and portfolio tool. Teachers can create one notebook per student and then curate their projects by taking photos of physical assignments, sharing digital ones via email to the student's notebook, recording student's thoughts and reflections with audio, and typing additional notes for assessment purposes, to create a robust portfolio for each child. These student notebooks could then be shared with colleagues, peers, or parents.
>
> Similarly, students who have their own Evernote accounts (either free or premium) can use their own system of notes and notebooks to reflect on their learning. While Google Drive is an excellent tool for curating content and collaborating with others, the clean interface of individual notes and notebooks, combined with the audio and photo note features, gives students a quiet place to think about their progression as learners.

Conclusion

We're excited about four things that educators are doing to help students read and consume content using iPads and transform the collection process: First, teachers are taking a print-disabled curriculum and finding ways of using the iPad's Accessibility features and various apps to provide more pathways into course content for students. Second, teachers are integrating more diverse forms of media into the curriculum and thereby allowing students to access content through print, audio, video, simulation, and more. Third, teachers are exploring more ways of teaching increasingly common modes of reading, including both deep, focused reading and a form of reading that draws together threads from many different modes. Finally, teachers have their students interacting with text in new ways—annotating, taking notes, and, increasingly, organizing ideas across texts and sharing their ideas across different groups.

Students having access to diverse materials that are personalized to their capacities and interests not only creates exciting opportunities; it also opens up a new problem: How do you organize all of these resources, and feeds of new resources, so they can be cataloged, used, and understood most effectively? To answer that question, we turn to our next chapter: "Curation on the iPad."

2 Curation on the iPad

Like most of us, Instructional Technology Specialist Daniel Callahan isn't a big fan of a lot of the email he receives, but on occasion he receives a message in his inbox that makes him smile. "Every once in a while I get an email because a second grader wrote something in Google Drive and they shared it with me—and not because they were working on something with me, but because they wrote something and they were proud of it and they wanted to share it with me," Dan said.

It's moments like these that comprise Dan's greater argument for using iPads in the classroom. Next year, his Burlington Public School district in Massachusetts will become entirely one-to-one, or one iPad per student. He has helped implement iPads gradually: the first year with fourth and fifth grade, and this year with first grade. On a given day, Callahan can walk the halls and see the effects: first graders researching the solar system by watching videos on their devices, fourth graders using math apps to practice skills, a fifth-grade class writing in Google Drive. In all of this, Dan bears witness to the ways iPads foster curation and connection—both in the digital realm and in the physical world.

"Part of the way [the iPad] has helped build community is that it's been a really great learning experience for teachers and students, especially in the first year, when we were piloting. They were all in it together," Dan said.

Technology, particularly Google Drive, has become a central part of day-to-day communication. Within the Google Drive app, students can create folders, documents, and spreadsheets that can all be shared and worked with collaboratively—in real time directly or asynchronously—from an iPad. Students working in groups have the ability to not only create a Google Document to collaborate on the writing process, but they can also upload PDF files (and other file types) to a collaborative folder. "Google Drive has been an absolutely essential part of keeping everybody connected and working together, or really the whole Google suite," Callahan said.

Schools like Dan's realize that curation—the intentional selection, organization, and maintenance of works or artifacts—is an increasingly important skill in the digital world. With the wealth of knowledge and information accessible through a network connection and a few taps, students must not only be able to navigate and evaluate what they find but also be able to curate effectively. With information at the user's fingertips and apps that allow for interaction, shelving, tagging, and personalization, the iPad can allow students to create an organized network of learning resources that can be seamlessly integrated with the resource networks of other students and teachers.

Most museums and art galleries have a curator whose job it is to collect and annotate exhibits for viewing by the public. Only a fraction of a museum's collection is available for viewing at any one time. It is the curator's job to know about each of the various pieces in the collection and to be able to categorize them in various ways. He or she might pull out only pieces that were created with stone tools for a pre–Iron Age exhibit, for example, or feature different pieces that depict humans' relationship with nature for an exhibit on the environment.

The job of the curator is thus essential. He or she must have a broad range of knowledge about many different pieces and styles in order to create exhibits for visitors. The curator does not have to be an expert practitioner in the area he or she is curating. After all, no one can be an expert in everything, and if someone were truly an expert in archaeology, he or she would probably be out in the field actually doing archaeology. Rather, a curator must be an expert in guiding the experience of the visitor in the museum gallery—he or she should know where the visitor is likely to get lost and understand how to convey the right amount of information at any given time.

As teachers, we should similarly be curators of information about our subject. Many people erroneously believe that the highest qualification that a teacher can have is to be an expert in his or her field. While some content expertise is always good, it is much more important that teachers are experts in guiding the experience of the learners in their classrooms by helping to select and curate resources that are personalized to individual learners.

In his recent book *Truth, Beauty, and Goodness Reframed*, Harvard professor Howard Gardner (2001) argues for the importance of curation in learning to appreciate beauty. He states that the abundance of great art and literature, and our access to them, has destabilized the notion of a fixed set of canonical works. In an interview about the book, Gardner explained, "We're no longer going to have a single canon where a central authority will be able to decide what's great and what's not . . . Everybody can make his or her judgments about beauty, and it doesn't impinge on anybody else" (Sweeney, 2011). To develop our own canons, to learn to appreciate beauty, he recommends maintaining portfolios or journals of art, music, writings, and experiences in order to better appreciate the distinctions among them and to make sense of which pieces are most beautiful.

What would a math class look like where students learn to compute, prove, derive, and intuit, as well as discern and appreciate mathematical beauty? What about a history class where students maintain a portfolio of beautiful artifacts and ideas from multiple periods? How might efforts to curate benefit from the portability and ubiquity of mobile devices? What would a "relevance portfolio" look like, where students catalog their daily encounters with ideas or experiences? What other kinds of portfolios could students create over the course of their academic career?

In a world of informational abundance, we no longer face the ancient world's challenge of finding scarce information. In a world of portable supercomputers and ubiquitous access, the task of the teacher is no longer to collect and distribute but to empower students to curate their own collections of intellectual resources.

Advantages of Curation on the iPad

There are multiple advantages for students of curating content on the iPad. Curation on the iPad can move students beyond the limitations of pen and paper and help them take advantage of knowledge management in a multimedia, social, and mobile context.

Mobile Curation

Being able to collect on the go is one of the benefits of having a travel-size device. The ability to listen to a playlist of podcasts on the bus ride home or to take pictures during a parade to capture intergenerational community involvement for a civics class allows students to choose what they want to capture from the world around them in audio, video, images, or text. Apps that are tied to the classroom are also available anywhere that students are, and using Socrative, Edmodo, or Schoology, with their real-time updates, promotes a current, up-to-date, and connected learning experience. Breaking down the walls of the traditional classroom through time gives students the opportunity to own the pace, time, and place of their learning, and provides opportunities for greater engagement.

Engagement

Visually appealing apps and texts help people not only understand content but also personalize their interaction with an app. Instagram's various filters encourage people to alter their photos, and in providing a choice of effects, the program gives people a creative outlet for their photos. Students could use the filters to capture the tone and mood in poetry or from a character, or to take photos that capture a certain democratic ideal in social studies class. In addition, the multimodal elements of apps help students engage with topics, thus synthesizing their understanding of the material and appealing to different types of learners. The TEDEd app gives users options to engage with videos through paired quizzes, notes, and discussions. Integrating multimodal elements into the app promotes pairing multiple modalities like audio, video, and text, which in turn reinforces students' understanding of the anchor text.

Functionality

Having apps that not only support one another but are also easy to use is key to facilitating curation on the iPad. Apps that allow users to alter text, images, and sound allow them to experience the material in a way that best suits their learning. Curation is facilitated both by collecting content within particular apps and by transferring content between them, in that students can capture in one setting and refine their thinking in another. The critical thinking skills required to not only juggle those processes but also to send content to another app or collection area—by bookmarking, annotating, or emailing it to return to later—are a key element of curation in the overwhelming information society of the 21st century. Teachers must not only teach students critical skills in using apps but also lead them to understand the ways in which they learn best. It is also important that they help students help themselves in terms of the type of media they use.

Social Curation

Navigating social networks to gather information is a valuable way to leverage crowdsourced knowledge and information. Finding out what people have already discovered, what they have written about, and what they are interested in is embedded in the social fabric of human relations. Apps that rely on social networks (e.g., Twitter, Facebook, Diigo, and Pinterest) and leverage collaborative interaction to expand understanding and participate in problem solving are an important functionality to have in the 21st century. To that end, embracing social collaboration expands students' exposure to diversity—an important element of truly being a digital citizen.

Beyond the myriad ways that the iPad is a tool of consumption, it is, more importantly, a tool of curation. From the design of how its apps function to the ways they are designed to facilitate learning, curation on this device embraces the interdisciplinary nature of teaching and learning.

Managing Files and File Types on an iPad

In order to reach lofty heights of thoughtful curation, teachers and students need to understand some of the mechanics of managing different files and file types online using an iPad. Most students are familiar with using word-processing document formats like Microsoft's .doc and .docx to create texts and the Portable Document Format, or .pdf, to read texts. When using iPads, there are three file formats that students should be familiar with: the .doc, the .pdf, and the .epub, the latter being a flexible platform for multimedia creation. Understanding what each file type can do is essential. Their capabilities are summarized in table 2.1.

Table 2.1: Capabilities of the Different File Types

File type	Capability
.doc OR .docx	Flexible file types that can be opened by word-processing programs; editable.
.epub	Flexible file type that can be opened by e-reader programs like iBooks and Kindle; can contain multimedia.
.pdf	Static file type that can be opened by annotation programs, iBooks, and other varied apps; limited multimedia options.

EPUB files are becoming increasingly popular on mobile devices and provide a rich multimedia reading experience. They can contain audio, video, and images, as well as dynamic text (meaning that words can be clicked or tapped to activate speech-to-text, annotation features, dictionaries, and so forth). The types of interactive and animated features that one finds in an Inkling book are a product of this technology.

On the other hand, PDF files provide a "flat" surface to which students can add elements. For instance, they can highlight, type, and draw on top of a PDF document. They can even record audio, depending on the tool that they use. Some annotation tools allow PDF files to be combined with webpages that can be opened in a browser.

A .doc file is a Microsoft Word document file format. In 2007, .docx replaced .doc as the default Microsoft Word file format, though one can still create and save .doc files. You must use an appropriate app to open Microsoft Word files, such as the Microsoft Word app or Apple's Pages. Microsoft Word file formats are flexible, so teachers and students can create and edit in a multimedia, word-processing environment.

By having a fuller understanding of the differences in the file types, teachers can be more specific in how they have students interact with information. The EPUB file type provides more interactive consumption and curation potential but is in much less circulation than the PDF file type and can be opened in fewer apps. Although the PDF is in greater circulation than the EPUB, it has less interactive and multimedia potential.

Due to its widespread usage and ubiquitous compatibility, we will primarily focus on the PDF file type for the duration of the chapter. For both teachers and students, there is a tremendous amount of curriculum content in the form of books, articles, papers, reports, and more available as PDFs. The PDF is a ubiquitous file format and is used extensively in K–20 online publications, so searching expressly for pedagogical and curriculum content available in PDFs makes sense. As far as the iPad, there is a very important reason why teachers and students should search for online books, articles, papers, and reports as PDFs: there are many iPad apps that can open a PDF file, so using this format will give students many engaging ways in which to interact with information.

Many iPad apps have features for content consumption and creation compatible with PDF documents. In one instance, a PDF file could be annotated with notes and comments and combined with a webpage that includes such features as a video tutorial, a slide show, or a podcast, as seen in figure 2.1. In another instance, an image could be added to the file, graph, or chart. Essentially, a small icon representing a webpage could sit somewhere unobtrusively on a PDF document and be tapped to open the page. In these ways, students can bring in the world's information to the PDF document.

As we said in the introduction, the challenge for educators is not in learning to use the iPad or apps. The real challenge is in imagining innovative learning environments that can augment, or even redefine, student learning.

So, imagine the potential of students being able to bring webpages and audio recordings into their notes alongside conventional note taking. Think of students being able to insert extra pages between notes of a math problem or a video tutorial to remind them how to solve the problem. Students could also record their thoughts as audio before (or after) attempting to solve the problem and add the audio to their notes.

Consider also the power of a student leveraging both speech-to-text and text-to-speech functions in order to engage with, and gather needed information from, what would otherwise be a completely inaccessible piece of paper. Imagine a reading assessment during which students practice active reading strategies on a PDF while recording themselves reading the passage aloud or a writer's workshop where they insert

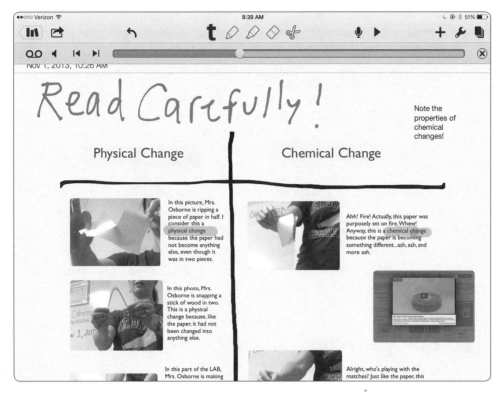

Figure 2.1: iPad screen where an audio file and a movie, along with notes and highlights, have been added to a PDF file to annotate the document.

PDFs into a screencasting app and then provide their peers with video feedback. Whereas on computers the PDF format is generally used for consuming content, on an iPad a PDF serves as a jumping-off point for many different active-learning possibilities.

In Douglas Kiang's computer science class at the Punahou School in Hawaii, students use PDFs regularly and work in a collaborative group to create a final project.

Here is how Douglas explained it:

> My job is to assess the process of their work over a period of time. Students create PDFs on their iPads as they work. Every day, students file a "work log"—a short accounting of their time spent working on the project.
>
> By sharing their PDFs with each other, students get a sense of what progress is being made on different parts of the project. Twice a week, students write journal entries reflecting on the progress of their learning. These are also saved as PDFs from their iPad and shared with me.
>
> Instead of a final exam, students are asked to write a narrative about the process they went through to create their final project; in effect, to "tell me the story" of the semester's work. However, they can't make

up any details; they have to cite their sources, and their primary source material is drawn from the very work logs and journal entries they have been curating all semester on their iPads.

Once students turn in all of their final narratives, which can be three to five pages long, I can keep all of them as PDFs on my iPad. I read through them using iAnnotate (an annotation app), and leave comments for them in the body of the document. I then save those comments right into the PDFs, and email the PDFs back to the students. Because the comments are embedded in the PDF file itself, my students can read the comments on their notebooks or iPads.

Douglas and his students incorporate PDF files as an effective way of collecting, sharing, organizing, and commenting on information. Thinking back to Ben Shneiderman's CRCD framework, the students in Douglas's class collected information and related to one another in unique ways via the iPad. He has developed a system of curation and connection whereby student work is not only organized but shared actively between the teacher and the student and from student to student.

iPad PDF Collection Activity

Here is a simple activity that you can do to illustrate the ability to collect educational PDF files on an iPad:

1. Perform a web search for the educational content in a PDF format. For instance, a history teacher might perform a "United States Constitution PDF" Google search.

2. When the search results come up, tap on a "United States Constitution PDF" result that has "[PDF]" in the upper-left-hand corner preceding it.

3. Now, tap anywhere on the PDF file and look for an Open In button to appear in the top-right corner of the document, as shown in figure 2.2.

4. Tap the Open In button.

These simple steps enable a PDF document to be opened in any number of apps, ready for student interaction. In this example, students would instantaneously have a primary source document on their iPad and be able to interact with it in multiple ways. They could open up the PDF document in an annotation app, such as iBooks or Notability, and immediately begin taking notes on the document. Or they could open it up in an audio-recording app, such as AudioNote, and create a recording to add to the document. Another option would be for students to open the PDF up in a presentation app like Explain Everything and create a multimedia presentation

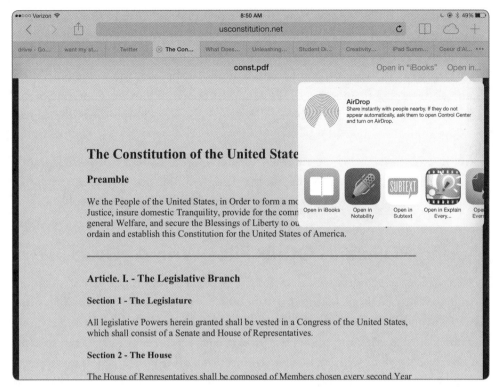

Figure 2.2: Tapping on a PDF document in a Web browser reveals the Open In option.

about the document. They could also open up the file in the Skitch image-editing app and create a drawing, or callouts, to accompany the document. Additionally, they could open the document in Evernote, tag it, and then store it in a Notebook. With an iPad, students can store all of their notes and handouts in one place on the web—so no more of the "I forgot my notebook" excuse!

Annotating and Notability

Annotating texts has been a central part of developing and demonstrating understanding in the humanities for thousands of years. It is a regular activity in many classrooms, and the process adds value, clarification, and information to a resource. From notes on a recipe calling for more sugar to a personal reflection on a metaphor in a piece of literature, commentary provides information for evaluating an experience. On the iPad, annotation apps not only mimic the paper act of annotation but also provide transformative opportunities that students can't find with pen and paper.

While there are many annotation apps, the one that we currently recommend is Notability. Notability is a powerful digital note-taking app and an outstanding PDF annotation tool. It allows users to create digital paper that can include text, freehand writing, images, illustrations, graphs, charts, audio, webpages, and more. Notability combines the ability to annotate PDFs with the opportunity to create original notes and word processing all in one. Notability Notes can be exported from the app to Dropbox and via email as PDFs.

Visit http://edtechteacher.org/tutorials/notability for an EdTechTeacher video tutorial on using Notability to annotate on the iPad. (All links for this book are also at www.learningsciences.com/bookresources and edtechteacher.org/ipadbooklinks.)

Sharing PDFs and Other Files With AirDrop

As Greg Kulowiec, senior associate with EdTechTeacher, points out, one of the most exciting new features available starting with iOS 7 is the ability to AirDrop files from one iPad to another, or even from one iPad to many, instantly. While sharing options that already exist, AirDrop makes the process easier and faster in that the sharing can take place with or without a Wi-Fi connection and from any app that supports exporting files with the traditional iPad Action or Sharing button (arrow pointing up from a small box on iOS 7 and later).

The major limitation of AirDrop is that it is only supported on the fourth-generation iPad and iPad mini. However, using AirDrop is fairly simple. For example, all you have to do to reveal the menu and turn on the feature is to swipe up from the bottom of your iPad with one finger. The option also exists to limit which AirDrop-enabled iPads can see your device by allowing you to select specific contacts. When a file is dropped from one iPad to another, the recipient also has the option to accept or reject the file. If the file is accepted, any potential application that can be used to accept it will be listed for the recipient to choose. AirDrop sharing is based on the proximity of devices, as they need to be able to find one another via Bluetooth.

Visit http://edtechteacher.org/tutorials/airdrop for an EdTechTeacher video tutorial on how to AirDrop materials from iPad to iPad.

Have an older iPad without AirDrop? Don't fret. We discuss sharing content with Google Drive in the next chapter on creativity.

Saving Documents as PDFs

Ask any teacher how many of his or her course materials—syllabi, homework, readings, and so on—are saved as Word documents (or on another word-processing platform), and chances are they have a lot. Well, Word documents, and many other types of Microsoft Office or iWork documents, can be converted easily to a PDF. This gives you the opportunity to convert custom content into digital formats for students to consume.

In most cases, one can simply select Save as PDF in the Save menu. Once saved as a PDF, teachers can move their PDF documents onto their iPad as well as their students' iPads. So instead of printing out dozens (hundreds?) of paper copies for students (that are often lost), teachers will have PDF copies at the ready to disseminate speedily onto iPads.

Using PrintFriendly

PrintFriendly.com offers an easy-to-install bookmarklet (a bookmarklet is a bookmark that users can save on a web browser in order to add new features or functionality) that transforms non-PDF webpages into PDF files. PrintFriendly also gives users the option to include or exclude photos on the site, or even to delete specific paragraphs. So in addition to converting the file, it can strip out unwanted advertisements and navigation elements. If a resource is too long or if a teacher wants to narrow down the reading of a page to a specific section, this feature provides the option to personalize the content before creating the PDF. With this convenient tool, teachers can convert articles to PDFs for students to read as homework, and students can have the flexibility to choose how they want to engage with online resources to support their own learning.

If you need to translate a website into an EPUB file, dotepub.com also provides a free bookmarklet that makes it possible to import webpages directly into iBooks. A featured article on Science Friday from NPR, for example, can now become a static document that students can highlight, and draw upon, or import into iBooks. Once in iBooks, students can access the associated dictionary as well as compile and export their own list of highlighted quotations. Figure 2.3 shows the URL for a *Science Daily* article pasted into a URL text box on the PrintFriendly website to be converted into a PDF document.

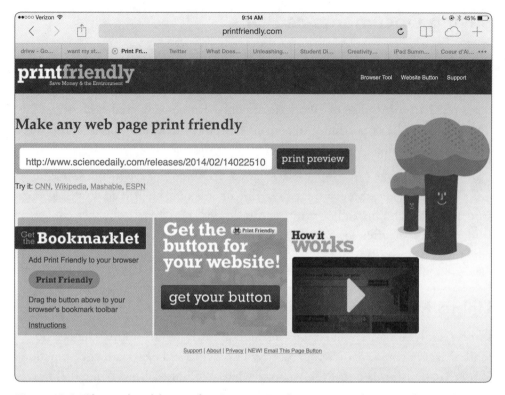

Figure 2.3: The web address of a *Science Daily* news article pasted into the PrintFriendly website to turn it into a PDF document.

Curating Websites With the Safari Browser and Home Screens

The iPad has some organization features that you can commonly find through a Safari browser search by using bookmarks and the Bookmarks bar. With the Action button of the browser, it's easy to create new bookmarks or add to the Bookmarks bar. Students can bookmark a class blog or online citation resources like EasyBib. When you tap the Bookmark icon, a drop-down appears with a list of webpages that have been bookmarked, as shown in figure 2.4.

There is also the option of selecting the Add to Home Screen option for a particular web address, as shown in figure 2.5, which creates an icon on the iPad desktop with a shortcut to that web address. Tap the Share icon in the top-right corner of the screen and then tap Add to Home Screen.

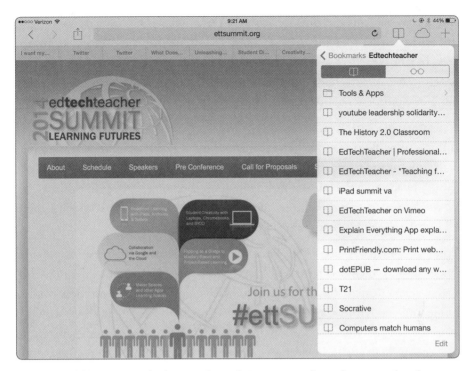

Figure 2.4: When tapped, the Bookmark icon reveals webpages that have been bookmarked.

Figure 2.5: You can select the Add to Home Screen option for a web address or tap the Share icon to bookmark a webpage on the iPad.

In this way, students can directly access resources like a class blog or learning management site without having to enter (and potentially misspell) the URL in Safari's address bar. For teachers who update their resources often, this creates a more direct connection between teacher, student, and information, as the only step involved is tapping on a home screen icon.

If comfortable with quick response (QR) codes, teachers can transform a URL into this scannable code and then redirect where it goes—so if they want to set up a math link for their students, they can change what resource it directs the students to simply by tapping the corresponding icon on the home screen. In this way, handouts, websites, and even peer presentations can appear on every iPad with minimal workflow juggling by the student.

Other web browsers have other benefits that supplement (and even supplant) the Safari browser. Downloading the Chrome app allows you to sync all open Chrome browsers across devices. So, if your students were doing research on their computers at home and wanted to transfer their pages directly to their iPad, they would only need to sync the devices. In addition, using Google Cloud Print, students can "print" documents to their iPad, providing an immediate digital photocopy of any resource that would otherwise be printed on paper. This has powerful workflow implications, as students can hand in their work by printing it to their teacher's iPad or share peer drafts directly with one another. Like any workflow solution, using Google Cloud Print needs some account management and prototyping before it is rolled out in the classroom.

Customization

When organizing broader and shorter reading selections by interest, apps such as Flipboard and Zite provide customized reading experiences. By leveraging touch-screen capabilities, these apps allow students to read traditional newsstand-style magazines in an interactive manner filled with content that is personalized according to the student's choice and social connection as well as RSS (real simple syndication).

With Flipboard, students can swipe through an interactive space that is made up of content from their social media timeline, adjust the feed so that it follows subject-specific topics, enlarge pictures, or expand the content so that they can view full articles and posts. Combining the images and text of online content with the kinesthetic experience of flipping through a magazine feels more rewarding than scrolling through a long vertical timeline. Figure 2.6 shows a page in the Technology section of Flipboard's app.

Figure 2.6: Page in the Technology section of the Flipboard app.

Zite, a similar online compilation app, exposes readers to a variety of articles based on a broader range of topics. In Zite, students can choose to explore a variety of posts and articles on a topic of interest. In this way, the reading experience becomes about social breadth rather than a specific set of people. Metaorganization apps like this one pull from various sources, accessing articles beyond what immediate feeds might give students and providing them with a more global reading experience.

With both Flipboard and Zite (as well as similar apps such as Feedly or Pulse), collecting content becomes much more than reading feeds and gets into flipping through a visually engaging medium of personalized content. In addition to consuming text, all of these apps include embedded video and audio, allowing students to take advantage of the associated multimedia integrated into the articles. Learning becomes much more personal and productive when students are engaged and interested in the content in front of them.

Social Bookmarking on the Web and in the Cloud

In using existing social media curation tools, the act of intentional aggregation is modeled for students and they get an understanding of what that process means so they can distill it for their own purposes. Flipboard and Zite draw upon broad ranges of articles by topic and RSS feed, exposing students to resources potentially beyond their research scope or perhaps as an introduction to a new topic.

When they are learning to curate social media, students might search a topic and select three resources—one about something they already know and two that teach them new information; for instance, they might start with a unit about DNA, activate prior knowledge, and then learn something new. Pairing an iPad with activities and questions like this helps to guide a purposeful search for information, reinforcing existing knowledge and encouraging differentiation and interest in finding new facts.

Social media tools become particularly useful within the connected reading context as students bounce between websites and media outlets. Some students may use the online social bookmarking tool Diigo in order to utilize the annotation tools and contribute notes to a Group. (Visit http://edtechteacher.org/tutorials/diigo for an EdTechTeacher video tutorial on how to curate websites using Diigo.) Others might use Evernote's Clearly or Web Clipper to save annotated webpages into notes and notebooks that can then be shared. With either of these options, annotations and texts can be accessed from any place at any time, creating a truly mobile experience.

Some cloud apps are more accessible than browser bookmarking. Evernote, Instapaper, or Pocket are all curation formats that you can send resources to from any app.

As mentioned in the last chapter, Evernote gives you an email address, so others can email content directly to your Evernote account. You can also use Evernote's Web Clipper tool to send your own email messages to one of your Evernote Notebooks. Personal or academic compilation is made easier through apps that can be organized and that you can return to and further refine at a later date.

Evernote has a few key features that help keep students organized in a variety of ways. First, typed notes can be organized into notebooks, either by subject or unit. In addition to being able to search the text of all notes, Evernote also searches any pictures or PDF documents. So if students have taken a picture of notes on the board or taken notes on a classmate's poster, they can also search and tag those notes. To help organize all of the information it aggregates, Evernote's platform uses tagging to organize information. Tagging a note with a keyword allows you to search by those tags. Table 2.2 shows the tagging keywords that might be used by Evernote for three separate notes.

Table 2.2: Potential Tagging Keywords Used by Evernote for Notes

Note	Potential keywords
Bill of Rights	law, constitution, control, rights, freedom
McCarthyism	fear, control, Communism, freedom, social control, constitution
Fahrenheit 451	social control, fear, violence, books, happiness, order

By searching the word *control*, all three of the notes in this example would come up, and students can take the time to consider how they are related. Not only does tagging encourage interdisciplinary organization, but it also helps students connect ideas across time in their school year. A search of violence might bring up the revolutionary guerilla tactics used in the United States as well as the nonviolent resistance of the civil rights movement. These types of cross-curricular connections can encourage students' critical thinking skills.

The following sections suggest a few other tools to consider.

Scoop.it

Scoop.it allows users to create and share their own themed magazines designed around a given topic, as shown in figure 2.7.

Here are three examples of courses and learning resources that have been built in scoop.it.

- Bioinformatics course: http://www.scoop.it/t/bs2064-bioinformatics
- Plant biology teaching resources: http://www.scoop.it/t/plant-biology -teaching-resouces-higher-education
- IT professional skills course: http://www.scoop.it/t/ct231-it-professional -skills-module

(All links for this book are also at edtechteacher.org/ipadbooklinks.)

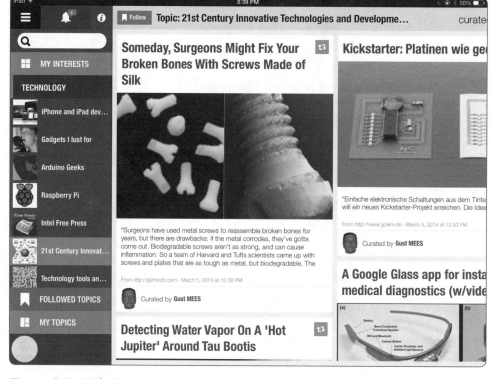

Figure 2.7: With Scoop.it, you can easily collect and share articles to create a themed magazine.

Pearltrees

Pearltrees is a content curation site that allows you to form communities by sharing links through a visually striking interface. In Pearltrees, students can add comments to pearls, essentially annotating the resource. For example, as a visual alternative to an annotated bibliography, they can add their source summary and analysis to the Comment feature.

Storify

When they want to create a narrative with multimedia aspects that will inform others, many students and teachers turn to Storify, a platform that integrates information from social media sites to tell the story. Curators can add text, photos, videos, and tweets to the story and then publish it to the web. Here are some examples of work done at the University of Alaska-Farmington.

- All about the Tundra Biome: http://storify.com/knewton/all-about
  -the-tundra

- Journalism: How to Make a Basic News Video for Web: http://storify .com/kellyfincham/how-to-make-a-basic-news-video-for-the-web

- Syllabus Constructed in Storify: http://storify.com/edwardboches /strategic-creative-development

Scoop.it, Pearltrees, and Storify represent a combination of linear and nonlinear collection tools. With these tools, teachers can model and share their own curation (on a class blog, through Twitter, or through other means), while students can learn about what the tool does.

The Why and the How

Every year, teacher Kristen Wideen creates a project and invites other classes to join in. This year, her third-grade classroom is using the Book Creator app to create an e-book about the global community. Visit http://leighherman.blogspot .com/2014/01/global-community-book-project.html to view the classroom video about the book students created on the global community with the Book Creator app.

What's really amazing is that students came up with the idea for this book based on Kristen's question, "What should we do?"

Kristen commented on the project:

> This year, in the grade 3 curriculum, students needed to learn about communities and the characteristics of different communities. Instead of doing the traditional unit, my students and I loved the idea of inviting other classes to contribute a page or two using the Book Creator app about the community where they lived.

> We created a video with sample questions, and the class tweeted it out on their classroom Twitter account, and I tweeted it out on my professional Twitter feed. I was shocked by the amount of people who wanted to participate in the Global Communities iBook Project. Teachers from Canada, Australia, the United States, Hong Kong, Scotland, and South Korea all signed up to participate. Pages poured in from around the world from students of all ages and all abilities. I asked teachers to save their pages in Dropbox and email me the link to their pages.

> Once the book is compiled, anyone in the world will be able to experience this amazing multimedia creation. It is filled with video, audio, images, and text from children around the world.

> This project has not only empowered my students to share their learning about their community, it has empowered hundreds of students to share something special about where they live. And they are so excited to know that they have an authentic audience of their peers anxious to see their creations.

So, you've reached the point where you and your students have found resources through social media, RSS feeds, or individual research on the web. What's the purpose? Is it for individual curation, out of your interests, or just for the sake of collecting? Is it to teach yourselves something or to teach others? Is it to convince someone of a point of view or to reveal a pattern or trace? Curation can fulfill many purposes, but as Kristen pointed out, it's one of the best ways to connect your students to the world. In the rest of this chapter, we provide a variety of examples of how iPads can play a role in projects that focus on collecting and organizing learning resources.

Joint Curation Between Teachers and Students

In her combined first- and second-grade class, Kristen uses iPads to capture her students' thinking processes while allowing them to work independently. She incorporates familiar physical objects and then leverages the iPad to record their learning processes.

For example, to reinforce the abstract thinking involved in comparing units of measure and size, Kristen has students measure books with dominoes. Though this activity could be completed without an iPad, integrating the device allows her to capture students' thinking and learning as well as to document their progression.

Kristen starts out by having two iPads for her elementary students. She focuses on sight words and does a formalized research study to prove their value for teaching and learning. Her classroom is based on the "open" concept—it has no walls. Two combined grades work together and collide in the library. While, at first glance, her classroom may look similar to that of others, there are the following key differences:

- *Students choose their morning activity.* When students enter in the morning, they can read, blog, or tweet. They work independently or in groups wherever they like.

- *Parents are invited in for a community read.* On Tuesdays and Thursdays, parents are invited in for "community read," or a time when parents and students can read together. This time also includes a "Let's teach our parents" component for helping acquaint parents with the technologically connected classroom. In doing this, it has eliminated much of the pushback about what is happening with iPads and technology, by bringing parents on board to understand the value of devices as an extension of learning.

- *All of the iPads have twenty apps or fewer.* None of the iPads in Kristen's classroom have more than twenty apps, and almost all of those on student iPads are used for content creation. (Fewer apps means less confusion for kids and more time for the teacher to focus on creative uses.) Once the students have developed some fluency with them, they can then choose the creation app to best meet their needs.

• *Curiosity is encouraged.* Students are encouraged to wonder, ask questions, and then blog, write, draw, or otherwise come up with unique ways to express their interests. There are always prompts available to spur kids' imaginations. For instance, creatures are always placed in the classroom for kids to explore: worms, slugs, frogs, bug catchers, and so forth.

Paperless Curation

Greg Kulowiec said the following about how he and English teacher Katrina Kennett curated information with students in a paperless, iPad-integrated classroom:

> Before we start the process, we had a conversation about the goals of this research process and why iPads would be a good fit. I think it is critical to have this conversation when not only integrating iPads but using any type of technology in the classroom. The two critical questions we considered were: (1) What are the goals and objectives of the paperless research process? (2) How can iPads enhance the process and allow for opportunities that would not be possible without these devices?

Keeping these two questions in mind, they outlined both the goals for the paperless research article and how the iPads would fit into the process.

The goals were:

1. Students will crowd-source their research to a collective research group.

2. Students will incorporate varied media types into their research: web-based text, traditional text, and audio and video.

3. Students will work collaboratively with their teacher and classmates on the research and writing process.

4. Students will become proficient in researching and writing for a digital environment.

5. Students will become proficient in an iOS environment.

6. Students will incorporate web-based content in their final research paper.

The reasons why iPads are important for this process are that they enable:

• Web-based research and social bookmarking

• Access to digital content (text, audio, video)

- PDF annotation and note taking
- A shared research process where an open-research environment between the teacher and student is created
- The ability to post research content to cloud storage accounts directly from the iPad
- The ability to publish content online directly from the iPad

Now that the goals and justification were established, it was time to outline and begin the technical setup to make sure the research process could be completed on the iPad. To conduct the setup, they worked through the following steps.

1. Install the following apps required on the iPad:

    Pages ($9.99)—Word-processing app for writing the rough and final draft

    Dropbox (free)—Cloud storage app for sharing research and writing

    Notability ($2.99)—App allowing students to annotate PDF documents, type notes, and annotate paper-based text research

    iTunes U (free)—An Apple media player and mobile device management system to play, download, and organize digital audio and video

2. Create a Diigo group.

3. Have students create Diigo accounts and invite them to create a class Diigo group.

4. Have students create Dropbox accounts.

5. Have students create a research folder and share the folder with the teacher.

The process took place over a three-week period, and Greg and Katrina took at least two days prior to introducing the iPads to have the students create Diigo and Dropbox accounts and go over the particulars of the assignment.

Because they were working in a shared iPad environment, the students had to log in and log out of their Diigo and Dropbox accounts every day. In the beginning, they anticipated that this would be a minor obstacle to overcome, and within a few days, it would simply become part of the process.

Each day, students exported their content to their Dropbox accounts. Greg and Katrina anticipated that most students would work in the Notability app to annotate, take notes, and organize their work. Each note set could then be exported as a PDF.

When students began working on their rough and final draft in Pages, the teachers also had them export their work each day to their Dropbox accounts. This step ensured that no work was lost; there is the potential for work to be deleted in this shared iPad environment.

Conclusion

Museums and independent collectors have been curating artwork collections for years, and digital curation has now become a universal part of the iPad experience. With its digital form allowing curation to happen at any time in any place and its cloud servers backing up information so that little is lost, the iPad provides one platform that fulfills many different collecting, annotating, and presenting purposes.

Collecting and consuming in the 21st century involves critical questioning and analysis skills. The mass overload of information on the Internet and in apps shifts the focus from consuming and memorizing information to figuring out when and where to focus on quality texts. Once interesting and pertinent resources have been found, considering how to preserve them so as to facilitate their use, rereading, and alignment with the curriculum requires students and teachers to work with higher-order thinking skills.

The refocusing of the classroom from content to curation also affects the teacher-student relationship by allowing teachers to build relationships with students in more personalized ways. Instead of placing the locus of learning on the content, learning now focuses on skill building. It is not necessarily about maintaining the lockstep curriculum at the "right" pace—the traditional process that has too often set teachers behind as they were forced to simply cover the material at hand rather than digging deeply into it.

Students and teachers build networks based on individual and shared interests. Building these networks helps leverage the power of social content and allows learning to go beyond the teacher-student interaction. Finding experts and learning from them is part of learning about any new topic, and the iPad facilitates this learning beyond the walls of the classroom. In this way, the classroom becomes the space for practicing independent and social learning—experiences that students will take with them well beyond formal schooling and as they go into the world.

What should students curate? In the spirit of Gardner's beauty journals (described in the introduction to this chapter), we should aim not just to help students get organized but to closely and intentionally examine what they read, watch, see, hear, and collect.

3

Creativity on the iPad: Innovative Performances of Understanding

For math teacher Dan Bowdoin, teaching one-step equations to sixth graders had always been an interesting challenge. The textbook's confusing explanations and jargon (like "isolate the variable and then show a proper check to verify the solution") made understanding one-step equations a daunting task for his students. So Dan decided his students would create their own books.

First, his students watched short videos about one-step equations. Then his students used the Book Creator app on the iPad (and complimentary apps) to create over 130 multimedia books that feature text, handwriting, images, audio, and video to show others how to solve one-step equations. You can view their creations online at www.youtube.com/watch?v=w6BoSDYMlIg.

By halfway into their first year using iPads, Dan's students were, in his words, "content creation kings." The one-step equation project had pushed them to gather information on their own, and the creation and sharing of solutions had motivated them to work harder. Moreover, creating the videos helped strengthen their acquisition and use of math vocabulary (with words like *inverse*, *isolate*, *check*, *verify*, *solution*, and *opposite*) throughout the year. The teacher had created a process that allowed students to take more ownership of the learning process and used the iPad to help create engaging and varied ways for students to demonstrate what they had learned.

As Dan's class demonstrates, an iPad can provide teachers and students with an opportunity to restructure the learning process in innovative ways. His students took ownership of the one-step equation learning process and used their iPads as powerful creation tools to skillfully redefine the manner in which they approached and controlled information, process, and product.

Seymour Papert (1980), the developer of the LOGO computing language, begins his landmark book *Mindstorms* with a story about a set of gears he played with as a child. He describes the tangible experience of working with gears as accelerating his understanding of physics in a way that would have been much harder with only books and lectures. Because of this, he refers to gears as "objects-to-think-with."

These gears inspired Papert's theory of constructionism, which holds that humans find it easier to construct understanding if they use objects to think with. Papert thinks of computers, with their flexible and multifaceted capacities, as one of the premier objects to think with. He suggests that concepts make more sense to young people when they can manipulate and engage those ideas for themselves, either in digital ways or by controlling objects in the physical world.

One simple way of explaining our pedagogical theory of iPads is to suggest that we don't want tablets to just become replacements for notebooks and textbooks but to instead be objects that students can use to think with. We want students to use them to construct understanding, to demonstrate their learning within their courses of study, and to mess around with the world.

The iPad, more than anything else, is a portable, multimedia creation device. It is a camera and video recorder that is small enough to carry around but big enough to allow for sophisticated input. In one device, it carries more media-production capacity than even the most sophisticated schools had access to only a few decades ago. (To watch Tom describing the potential of the iPad as a creation device, visit www.youtube.com /watch?v=Z2s_8XH7fDI). (All links for this book are also at www.learningsciences .com/bookresources and edtechteacher.org/ipadbooklinks.)

In her book *Teaching for Understanding*, Martha Stone Wiske (1998) and her colleagues at Harvard's Project Zero coin the phrase "performance of understanding." They argue that the most important capacities for young people to develop cannot be assessed with fill-in-the-bubble tests or canned assignments. There is no multiple-choice question that can assess a student's ability to collaborate with others effectively or his or her capacity to solve ill-structured problems. These important capacities can only be demonstrated in performance: you show collaboration by collaborating; you show problem-solving skills by solving novel problems.

More than anything else, we get excited at the possibilities of using the iPad as a tool for students to create performances of understanding, a tool to think with. At the EdTechTeacher iPad Summit in Atlanta, Jennie Magiera showed a video of a math student working through a problem on a screencasting app, talking aloud, and showing and recording his work. In a biochemistry lab class at Deerfield Academy, students used their iPads throughout class to take pictures and video recordings of the lab experiments, which later became key parts of their reports and presentations. In helping students learn to make inferences from poetry, Kristen Ziemke had her first graders draw their mental images from poems that she read. History classes at the

Hillbrook School in Northern California had students in period costumes dispersed across the campus recording short reenactments.

Some of these performances represent summative assessments that encapsulate weeks of work while others take up only a fraction of a class period or even just a moment. This represents a potentially major shift in classroom technology use. For many years, media creation that used technology meant a substantial investment of time and effort to reserve equipment, reserve lab space, and dedicate multiple class periods to record, document, and edit the footage. It took so long for laptops to boot up and for people to get logged on that once they were open, it made sense to use them for the whole period. But the ease of pulling iPads out for a quick task and then tucking them back under the desk means that we can think about media creation as either something extensive or something brief. Whether it is done as a multiweek project or in a few moments, we can have creation become a more regular part of the routine of classroom life.

So, turn on the iPad, tap open the camera app, take a picture of something in your learning environment, and share or save it. Creation starts there.

Student Creation: Moving From Goals to Apps

In workshops and presentations, we frequently get asked, "What can the iPad actually do?" We encourage folks to use a different language, one that positions people as the actors rather than the technology. "What can a teacher do with an iPad?" is the more appropriate question. Even more important, "What can our students do with iPads?" Whenever possible we want people acting upon iPads, rather than technology acting upon people, or just out there by itself.

Only when we put the people before the technology can we begin to consider what it is that we want people to do better. In a blog post, Beth Holland (2012) of EdTechTeacher poses the questions, "Why iPads?" and "Why technology?"

Beth answers her questions in this way:

- "Because I want my students to communicate in complex and modern ways."
- "Because I want my students to make their thinking visible."
- "Because I want my students to document their thinking as they work through a process."
- "Because I want my students to have multiple ways through which to interact with learning objects."

Those are ambitious goals, but do they translate into classroom practices, and how? Well, in a recent workshop, Beth was approached by an English teacher who wanted to know where to begin with iPads. Beth's response was to start the workshop with a set of content-specific learning objectives. For the English and language arts classroom, she suggested that the "because" might look something like this:

- "Because I want my students to demonstrate their knowledge of the parts of a story."

- "Because I want my students to master the concept of the story arc."

- "Because I want my students to make a personal connection with their text and then communicate that back to their peers."

- "Because I want my students to collaborate in order to better comprehend difficult texts or dramatic works."

Beth then showed the teacher how students could use iPads in support of these learning objectives by outlining a learning objective and then constructing a project to help students reach the objective, such as: "I want my students to demonstrate their knowledge of the parts of a story." In addition to learning the story elements, Beth argues that students learn to write a constructive review, assess the credibility of an author or source, create a sense of visual hierarchy for their information, and document their sources.

Movie Posters

One project that Beth used with her students is creating book posters, where students created a movie-style poster, like the one in figure 3.1, with which to advertise their book. Students were required to include the following elements on their poster: the title, the author, a representative image, a hook to get people to want to read the book, a quotation of a credible review, and a student review. They then added audio narration to their posters in which they explain the included elements and how they each relate to the book. They shared the final products with the teacher, who combined them all into a single video that comprises the work of the entire class.

Beth then chose apps for students to use that support their objectives: "While this could be created on paper or using a computer, with an iPad and apps such as Skitch, Visualize, or Text Here, students can quickly create, publish, and share their work. By integrating with the camera roll, these posters could eventually include audio narration with Fotobabble, be included in a book with Scribble Press or Book Creator, or added to a video project with iMovie or Animoto."

Figure 3.1: Movie poster created by one of the students in Beth's class.

Notice that Beth's first priority was not to find cool apps or tools selected primarily for their engagement factor. Apps were selected because they supported and aligned with a vision. She did not put the proverbial cart before the horse, selecting tools because she found them engaging and then formulating a learning objective. Apps played a purposeful role in the support of student learning.

Beth conceptualized various additional projects to meet the other ELA learning objectives. As she put it: "I want my students to master the concept of the story arc."

In addition to demonstrating their understanding of the key elements of the plot—problem, rising action, climax, falling action, and resolution—Beth is concerned that students learn:

- To incorporate imagery and sound with written elements
- To collaborate and communicate with their peers

- To search for and distinguish between media freely available from Creative Commons and that which is copyrighted
- To properly document their sources

Video Trailers

Beth also had students create one- to two-minute video trailers to advertise their book. Like with movie trailers, these videos need to draw the audience into the plot and introduce the characters and setting but not give away the ending.

One student created a *Nation* trailer based on the novel by Terry Pratchett using an iMovie on a computer. Other Web 2.0 tools could have been used, although it would have been nearly impossible to complete this project in a classroom setting using traditional nondigital tools. Furthermore, the simplicity of iPad apps like iMovie and Animoto combined with the iPad's built-in video recording and editing functionality allows students to engage in the entire process of moving from production to creation to publication without the need for additional equipment or extensive training. As Beth explained: "I want my students to make a personal connection with their text and then communicate that back to their peers."

In addition to asking and answering questions to demonstrate their understanding of a text, students in Beth's class learn:

- To prepare and deliver effective oral presentations
- To support their thoughts, opinions, and ideas with literature
- To independently work through a process of scripting, storyboarding, recording, and editing

Video Talks

By setting up video talks, Beth had students create videos of themselves discussing key elements of the book (not plot summaries), which they would then show the rest of the class. Since students used iPads for this project, they were able to record, edit, and publish from a single device. They could then incorporate their videos into future projects such as a multimedia report on a print book they were reading. While this could have been accomplished with in-class presentations, using video allowed for additional practice and provided a less-threatening environment for students who struggle with public speaking. As Beth put it, "I want my students to collaborate in order to better comprehend difficult texts or dramatic works."

In addition to identifying key quotations, references, and literary devices, as well as defining vocabulary in context, students learn:

- To collaborate with their peers
- To communicate with text, imagery, sound, and animation
- To present information in a clear, logical manner

Online Presentations

For each scene or chapter in the text, Beth had students create a short video presentation to identify key points, define relevant vocabulary, and make critical connections. These videos, when aggregated into a collection, provided students with a review of the overall text as well as a study guide to increase comprehension.

Giving students the ability to immediately incorporate pictures from their camera into the project and then publish them to the web makes the iPad an invaluable asset in this learning context. Again, while this could have been accomplished on a computer, the iPad simplified the process and expedited the time required to go from concept to publication.

So, Beth provides us with learning objectives and activities designed for the ELA classroom. But what could iPad activities look like in other grades and disciplines? How do we go about selecting the right apps?

iPad As . . .

As we suggested in the introduction to the book, we believe that education for young people in the digital age requires helping them use digital tools to access new forms of knowledge, to personalize their studies, to connect with people around the world, and to demonstrate their understandings in diverse ways. Choosing tools is important but not as important as supporting teachers in incorporating technology in thoughtful ways that empower students. Every conversation about technology needs to start with the question, What do you want your students to be able to do?

Toward that end, we have created a popular collection of annotated apps for teaching and learning at http://edtechteacher.org/apps, known as "iPad As . . . ." Unlike other lists that promote "cool tools" or lists of content apps by academic disciplines, our list is driven by specific learning goals that promote critical thinking, creativity, collaboration, and community mindedness. In a nutshell, our focus is on what kids can do and not so much on what teachers can teach.

The first screen you will see when you follow this link gives you a list of choices of what you want to have your students do, as shown in figure 3.2. Our annotated list outlines apps suited to the student performance and rated for "usefulness" and "ease of use." We also let you know if the app is free or not.

You might choose to have students:

- Share their perspectives through digital stories

- Become more efficient learners and communicators by organizing their resources

- Teach concepts to others through screencasts and video tutorials

- Perform their understanding of a topic by recording and editing video

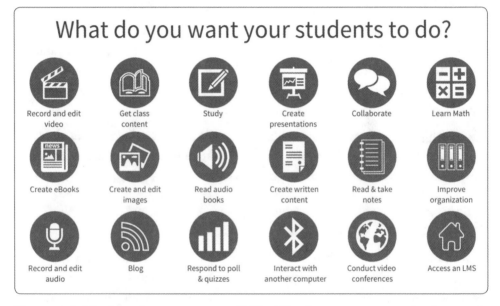

Figure 3.2: The learning resources at EdTechTeacher.org are organized around learning and teaching goals.

You might click the icon Create Written Content to bring up the link to the writing app that works with the device you're using, as shown in figure 3.3.

Figure 3.3: Reference entry about Notability from EdTechTeacher.org.

Armed with tools aligned to learning objectives, student performances on iPads can be both clever and creative. Figure 3.4 shows you the screen to get to the apps where you can record and edit video. Let's take a look at some of the projects students came up with using these apps.

First, let's watch a few minutes of an amusing video tutorial, where two high school science students use the Explain Everything screencasting app to create a "Puppet Pals" demonstration that shows their understanding of the relationship between altitude and temperature (https://www.youtube.com/watch?feature=player _embedded&v=3GRKjozn7J0). Next, let's take a look at a middle-school science project where students use the iMovie app to create a powerful video on food production (https://vimeo.com/61818515). Then, let's see how fifth-grade students at the Meadowbrook School in Weston, Massachusetts, create an animation of a counting poem (https://vimeo.com/59094126)—a novel way to explain a math concept. Finally, let's visit a kindergarten classroom where students create their own books using Book Creator and then ask their teacher if they can show another class how to do it themselves (http://www.redjumper.net/blog/2013/09/kids-teaching-kids -book-creator/)!

Figure 3.4: Video creation app recommendations from EdTechTeacher.org.

This approach, in which teachers start with goals and then think of which tools might fit, helps keep technology in the service of learning. Greg Kulowiec (2014) of EdTechTeacher described the process as:

> Start with the end goal in mind, the inspiration, the challenge, and then determine if an iPad can be used effectively, not to teach new content to students, but to allow them to achieve the end goal: to demonstrate their learning and share that understanding with their peers, a broader audience, and even potentially the world.

As we remind teachers, the challenge of integrating iPads into the classroom is not in learning how to use the apps. The challenge is in imagining the innovative ways in which the tool can be used to enhance student learning. It's to conceive of ways in which the iPad can be a pathway to new challenges, new creativity, new collaborations, new connections, and ultimately new opportunities for students to demonstrate and share their understanding.

One Screen

In our travels to various schools and districts, we are constantly struck by the number of apps that teachers and students put on iPads. In a trip to one elementary school, Tom swiped through screen after screen of apps that were nothing but games. Without a vision for learning with iPads, teachers had simply dumped game-playing apps onto iPads whose sole purpose was to "keep kids busy" when they were not involved in traditional classroom learning. At a secondary school, Tom encountered a tech integrationist who flashed screens full of "cool" apps during a presentation as she nervously raced through fifty apps during a thirty-minute presentation on how to use iPads in the classroom.

One of the core principles of effective iPad usage that EdTechTeacher has developed is the idea that educators should focus on creation apps rather than content apps. Most apps designed to teach specific content are "drill and kill." Instead of chasing and reviewing the thousands of education apps that come out every year, educators should consider how a small suite of apps related to annotation, curation, and image, audio, and video production could support diverse student performances of understanding. The eight apps shown in figure 3.5 provide many of the tools students need for content creation.

Figure 3.5: Only eight apps but untold active learning possibilities.

Overall, we hope that educators see that with a core set of evergreen apps covering a broad spectrum of consumption, curation, and creation, they have more than enough firepower to develop a full set of creative and purposeful lessons and activities. The material that teachers create will not only extend over the entire academic year but also generate what author and Harvard professor Tony Wagner terms "a culture of innovation," referring to an environment that encourages students to be the kind of adaptive, immersed thinkers and leaders essential for today's cognitively demanding and competitive global workforce.

Explain Everything: A Versatile Screencasting App for Creation

It's easy to fall prey to app chasing when you have neither a clear learning goal in mind nor a grasp of how one app could be used to unleash a myriad of active learning possibilities. Imagine for a moment that your superintendent suddenly dictates that you can only use one app on your iPad for teaching and learning. What would you do?

Well, consider that one app enables your students to do all of the following:

- Handwrite
- Type
- Draw
- Create images
- Create audio
- Create video
- Create animation

What could students do with one app that had all these capabilities? Quite a lot. They could write or type papers or reports. They could draw pictures and illustrate stories. They could make graphs or charts. They could make videos, including video tutorials. They could show others how to solve math problems. They could make slide shows and virtual posters. They could record themselves speaking a foreign language or playing the guitar. And the teacher could do all these things as well.

Explain Everything is an example of a screencasting app that can do all of this and more. Visit www.youtube.com/watch?v=ugMztuJyKyU for a video of middle school science students showing their understanding of plate tectonics in multiple ways using Explain Everything.

Screencasting apps (Educreations, ShowMe, and ScreenChomp are others) create a digital recording of a computer or tablet screen output and often contain audio narration. A screencast is essentially a movie of the product a user sees on a computer screen, enhanced with audio narration (the Khan Academy math video tutorials are perhaps the best-known example in education).

If we had our druthers, every iPad program in schools would begin with teachers only being allowed to use Explain Everything (or a similar app)—and nothing else—for the first month of classes. The idea is that if every teacher were to concentrate on maximizing the potential of one powerful and versatile app, his or her intellectual energies would be focused on nurturing active learning activities—instead of app chasing. At the same time, it could bring teachers across grades and disciplines together around a single app to brainstorm skill development activities and possibly foster interdisciplinary collaboration.

Where to Start? Targets of Difficulty

We've proposed an approach where teachers move from learning goals to specific apps and projects that can help students demonstrate their understanding. But where in the curriculum should a teacher start?

It's unlikely that any educator reading this book can take everything that he or she is doing, toss it aside, and start anew. Nor should he or she. For most educators, incremental change and iterative experimentation make the most sense. The idea of setting a "target of difficulty" can help educators decide where to start reforming their practice. A good target of difficulty is at the intersection of three conditions that you should determine.

The first condition to evaluate is the parts of the curriculum that are hard to teach. As far as that part of your curriculum where you are doing an awesome job and kids are learning in powerful ways—leave that alone. It's most helpful to experiment in the places where you are currently unhappy with how things are going or have gone in the past.

The second condition consists of the places in the curriculum that are important. You can experiment with a few areas to figure out what these are. Curriculum change is difficult, so invest time in the parts of your course that really matter, where students are working on the most worthy topics and the most enduring understandings.

The final condition is made up of the parts of your curriculum where technology might have some leverage. These are those places where you can imagine how having students perform their understanding in diverse forms of media would help solidify important understandings.

The intersection of these three areas—something that's hard to teach, something that is important to teach, and where technology will be helpful—is your target of difficulty. These targets are often great places for educators to start thinking about putting in the time and effort to create more opportunities for student creation.

A story from Tom's classroom, consisting of his revision of a unit on the Great Depression in US history, helps to illustrate what tackling a target of difficulty can look like (Reich & Daccord, 2009).

In years past, Tom found that the "alphabet soup" approach to teaching the Great Depression failed to engage his students. His tenth graders struggled to keep track of the NRA, the WPA, the TVA, and the other acronyms of the era, and worse still, the history of political bureaucracies dulled the drama inherent in this dark epoch. Searching for a new strategy, he stumbled upon the section of the PBS American Experience website about its movie *Riding the Rails*, which used multimedia stories, images, and recordings to reveal the experience of the 250,000 teenage hoboes of the Depression. Rather than using technology as an add-on, Tom redesigned his unit to let his students explore the Depression through the lens of teenagers just like, but also very different from, themselves. Tom redefined the unit's learning goal from "the ability to explain the federal response to the Great Depression" to "the ability to explain how impoverished teenagers navigated the social, economic and political conditions of the Depression." Based on that new goal, he developed a compelling, essential question: What was daily life like for teenage hoboes during the Depression?

Once Tom identified his learning goal, he used Shneiderman's CRCD framework, as diagrammed in figure 3.6, as a template for creating his new unit. CRCD projects begin with a chance for students to research and collect the factual building blocks of their learning project. From there, they relate with one another and work together in an effort to create a tangible demonstration of their understanding. They then donate their work to a public forum so that their learning can be of service to others.

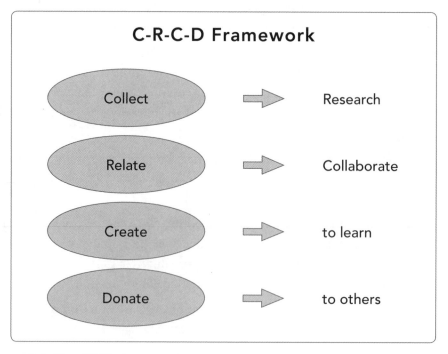

Figure 3.6: The CRCD framework.

Tom's unit began with an orientation to the 1930s using a typical set of readings, presentations, and discussions to provide context for the lives of young hoboes. The

Go to www.learningsciences.com/bookresources to download figures and tables.

"Day in the Life" project itself began with an opportunity for students to collect information about teenage hoboes. Rather than let students loose on the Internet, Tom guided his class to a group of well-chosen websites he found at EdTechTeacher's Best of History Websites site (http://www.besthistorysites.net). This guided inquiry included the aforementioned American Experience site, specific pages from the New Deal Network, and the National Heritage Museum's exhibition site on Teenage Hoboes in the Great Depression.

Students then created a fictional narrative about a teenage hobo, drawing on their historical research. They had a chance to relate to one another by commenting on and learning from each other's stories. After doing so, Tom told the class they would be producing a radio show, since the 1930s were known as the "golden age of radio." He then divided his students into roles: some would be the teenage hoboes getting interviewed, a few would be newscasters reporting from dust bowl states, one would give an FDR fireside chat on the plague of teenage homelessness, and another would supply a Republican response by Louisiana Senator Huey Long. He told them they had the rest of class to collectively research their roles, rehearse, and prepare. On the day of the radio show, Tom's classroom was abuzz with excitement and some anxiety. The students were about to be tested in a creative and fun but challenging oral assessment.

Tom's students used GarageBand, Apple's audio editing program, to create the radio show. While a few students went to quiet spaces to record their newscasts or fireside chats, Tom interviewed several small groups of student hoboes. He then compiled the students' recordings into a complete radio show. Using GarageBand, he compiled the individual pieces into a single audio file. He also used the app's prerecorded tracks to add intro music and sprinkle in applause. A few days later, he announced the show's debut, and again the room was filled with palpable energy. Students were both eager and nervous to hear themselves broadcast. Once the show started playing on the "radio," they listened with rapt attention as their classmates recounted their various perspectives on the social history of teenagers in the Great Depression.

During this final presentation, students had a chance to review the important historical concepts embedded in the radio show and take pride in the final product of their collaboration. The program remained available online so that students could revisit the show in preparation for the final exam or the AP American history test. Students also posted their stories and radio show clips on their blogs so that their classmates and school community members, as well as teachers and students from other schools, could learn from their work (see http://nobles.typepad.com /daccordus/). Students had a positive experience with academic service learning and enjoyed knowing that their efforts had a life beyond their notebook and the teacher's gradebook. (Much like Olivia years later remembering her Japanese cooking show assignment more clearly than any other lesson, Tom's students vividly recall the hobo project.)

The fine-grained historical detail that students used in their stories and interviews suggests that they collected important historical details from the Depression. They also demonstrated historical empathy for their teenage counterparts, recognizing the terrible conditions that young people faced in that era. In retrospect, Tom might have given students even more responsibility for learning by substituting the first few days of teacher-led lecture and discussion for student-led research and reporting, perhaps using a collaborative learning space like a Google Document.

It is in the *relate* category that the "Day in the Life" project has the most room for improvement. Having the collaborative relate work happen after the create work limited the potential for teamwork. While students used blogs to comment on one another's stories and added individual contributions to the radio show, more collaboration could have occurred if this work had begun earlier in the project. Students might have had the chance to cowrite the stories or radio show sections, perhaps using a document-sharing platform like Google Docs (www.docs.google.com) or to rewrite their stories after receiving online comments from peer editors.

Students certainly created engaging work products, both in terms of their stories and the characters they created during their interviews. In the early attempts at this project, Tom did most of the radio production work himself. In retrospect students could have taken on this responsibility. Classes might also work in teams to produce sections of the show or give a small group of technology enthusiasts extra credit for crafting a show from the raw tape. The more responsibility teachers can turn over to their students, the more the students will learn.

Since they built the project on a blogging platform, the students could easily donate their work to their colleagues and others outside the classroom. They benefitted from one another's work and were motivated to put forth their best effort by the project's public nature. Through sharing their stories, they learned that they didn't need to wait until adulthood to make intellectual contributions to a wider learning community.

Backward Planning Toward Products and Process

Thus far, we've suggested that student creation starts with goals and then turns to thinking about what kinds of products students can create. We want to add one more layer: educators should be intentional about guiding students through a structured process of creation.

In a post titled "4 Ways to Ensure Students Learn While Creating," history teacher and tech integrationist Shawn McCusker lays out his approach to facilitating project-based learning, which includes a focus on process (McCusker, 2013).

He begins:

> Education, guided by a focus on Bloom's Revised Taxonomy [see figure 3.7], is moving towards an emphasis on creation and innovation in the classroom. Though technology did not spark this movement, it has fueled the process by providing students with exciting and powerful tools. But is creation synonymous with learning? Can students even create without learning? How can we ensure that what they create has value?

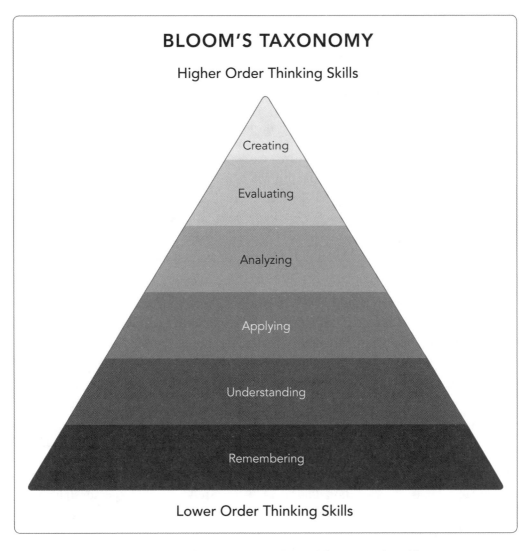

Figure 3.7: Bloom's Revised Taxonomy. Adapted from Krathwohl (2002).

Go to www.learningsciences.com/bookresources to download figures and tables.

He suggests that teachers need to help their students move past the flashy excitement of the best creation tools and establish a laser focus on their learning objective. Student work should be an expression of learning, not just the mastery of a tool.

Shawn proceeds to lay out his four main prompts for creative learning:

1. *Start with your specific learning objective.* Define the objective of your lesson clearly and effectively, then communicate it to your class. Allowing your students to have freedom and choice is much easier when those options revolve around a clear mission. Framing that mission for your class is where it all begins, and if done incorrectly, it is where things can come undone.

2. *The idea to be expressed should come before the tool used to express it.* In reality, all products are, in essence, an essay expressed through different mediums. Whether you call it a "main idea," a "thesis," or something else, all student projects should begin with one. This is the student's unique take on demonstrating the class objective and should guide his or her research and organization as well as his or her choice of tool.

3. *Make asking, "How will this show mastery of the learning objective?" your classroom mantra.* Repeating this will help students keep the assignment on track and evaluate the effectiveness of their work, which allow them to reflect on their current knowledge. This constant articulation of the learning objective in their own words also develops a crucial metacognitive skill: the ability to evaluate their own progress.

4. *Evaluate the students' process of creation rather than just grading the finished product.* Technology creates well-polished products. At first glance, a well-edited video or visually pleasing presentation can impress, but upon further evaluation, it may be of little substance. Creating check-ins and opportunities for peer and teacher review can keep the learning objective in view as well as support the development of skills. Watching how a student constructs meaning, formulates how to express it to an audience, and, only then, how he or she creates a presentation offers more opportunity to foster growth than just collecting an assignment ever will.

The industrial revolution song at https://soundcloud.com/shawn-mccusker /wh-dan-g-industrial-revolution illustrates how one student chose to demonstrate his mastery of the learning objective "Describe and communicate the ideas and philosophies that arose in response to the industrial revolution."

As Shawn emphasizes, the process of creation is as important as the final product. It's important to monitor the development of the student's product creation process to ensure that skill development and critical thinking are fundamental and continual.

Suggestions for Structuring the Student Process

Structuring the student process to meet learning objectives is critical. Here are some suggestions as to how to do so:

1. *Consider having students start offline.* One way to ensure that students stay focused on the ideas in the technology projects, rather than on the flash and sizzle of the medium, is to start by taking the technology away. When creating a multimedia project, it's often best to start with a nontechnology-oriented process. Having students use pen and paper and Post-it notes can help them get a handle on working through the planning process as they set up a tutorial video, a scripted podcast, or a simple slide show presentation. Through creating pen-and-paper outlines, storyboarding, and other processes, students can demonstrate the critical-thinking decisions that went into their multimedia production. They can then use the tangible artifacts of their process to show the teacher what they've contributed to the project.

2. *Have students working collaboratively use Google Drive.* If students are working through the intellectual process with others, then using a collaborative platform like Google Drive can help them to both synchronously and asynchronously participate in the construction of the intellectual work. For example, if two partners are creating a presentation on Vincent van Gogh, then they might work side by side to construct the outline, add their individual responsibilities at night for homework, and the next day do the editing in class together. They could give the final presentation to the class and record it with Explain Everything, and then publish the tutorial to YouTube and embed it on the class blog. In this way, their presentation won't just be on their Google Drive account; it will be captured for classmates and themselves to refer back to.

3. *Have students working individually create something to share (a lesson, an article for a class book, etc.) using the established platform that they normally use.* For example, they can use Explain Everything to annotate an excerpt from a text that the class is reading and then publish it to their YouTube or the class YouTube channel. Or they might take a stop-motion video demonstrating the physics of water ripples when a rock drops into a

pool with a voiceover to explain what physics theories are being proven in the video. Whatever the combination of multimedia elements, when students create to share with others—to teach them, to demonstrate their learning—the audience they are creating for will help determine what app they're using.

If brainstorming for an essay or other project, or to create a graphic organizer, students can use the app Popplet Lite to easily create a bubble map. This app allows more-visual learners to organize content in relation to other content, add different colors or shapes to the elements, and add "flash thoughts" as they make connections.

When composing an essay, the iPad can be an essential tool throughout the entire writing process. Google Drive can be used by individual students to set up documents for brainstorming, the outline, and the rough draft, as well as to provide a space to edit the final draft. The Revision History feature, available in the browser version, enables teachers and students to see the various iterations of a document, reducing the need for creating multiple files from the same document. If someone inadvertently or maliciously deletes any of the work, it is easy to revert to an earlier version and restore the document.

Since Google Drive is both a free collaborative platform and a free storage platform, it is ideal for collaborative projects. Since the service syncs with the cloud, it is also a convenient option for accessing content in different places on different devices.

To share work with students, a teacher can create a shared folder in Google Drive and give students access to the folder. To share work with a teacher, a student can create a shared folder and give the teacher access. Everything put in a shared folder is accessible to everyone added to that particular folder.

Apps With Cloud-Based Services

Fortunately, many apps allow you to upload the content you create directly to Google Drive and other cloud-based services. For example, content created in Explain Everything can be uploaded directly to a Google Drive folder. A Book Creator file can also be uploaded directly to a Google Drive folder, as can documents created in Notability. (Visit http://edtechteacher.org/tutorials/drive-notability for an EdTechTeacher video tutorial on using Notability with Google Drive.) (All links for this book are also at www.learningsciences.com/bookresources and edtechteacher .org/ipadbooklinks.)

Google Forms

Google Forms is a great tool for students to use when they want to track their thoughts or process over a period of time or subject unit. While the form itself has to be created on a computer, students can fill it out on an iPad, which feeds directly into a Google Spreadsheet that they can access on an iPad. If there is a consistent, quick writing activity, like a do-now or take-away routine, students can set up a form, fill in each day's prompt, and then compile the responses for the teacher to review at the end of the week. Alternatively, they can share the spreadsheet with the teacher continuously if they give him or her constant access. By using the iPad as a facilitation tool for ongoing work, students can more easily track their progress in an ongoing manner and cumulatively assess it later.

Collaborative Writing Apps

The collaborative writing and summative writing processes can both be undertaken effectively using the iPad. Using writing apps like Google Drive and Pages to produce and publish longer pieces of writing promotes the use of the iPad as a mobile, anytime writing device. This is important since students need to not only write for themselves and sometimes compile that writing for the teacher but also share their work and demonstrate what they know in more summative and formal mediums.

If writing collaboratively, the Google Drive app has a real-time collaboration feature that allows students to share their documents and read through them together, with each peer adding highlights and/or comments on the strengths and weaknesses of the other's paper. In the browser version of Google Drive, teachers can see which collaborators have added which content, providing a safeguard if they think students may have done unequal amounts of work on a document.

If students have shared their document with the teacher, then the teacher can access and comment while the students write and revise. This makes it easier to conduct miniconferences with students, as teachers can pull the student's paper up on their iPad, highlight sections and make a comment or two, and then move on to the next student's paper. Being able to give that real-time feedback makes the learning moments more powerful.

If students have written their work in the Pages app, then they can send it straight to a Dropbox or Google folder (that the teacher has access to) or email their teacher the document straight from Pages.

iPads and Video Feedback

For longer and more involved projects, it often makes sense for students to share drafts of their creations with other students.

Greg Kulowiec detailed a workflow for helping students to comment on each other's research papers. He suggested that students begin by outlining the process to put it in perspective in the following ways:

1. They use Google Drive to write their paper.

2. They share their Google document with the teacher to receive real-time digital feedback in the form of edits or inserted margin comments.

At the point where the students have a rough draft ready for peer editing, Greg suggested that students can take the next steps:

1. They share their rough draft Google document through Google Drive. The creator of the document only needs to provide viewing status, and the peer feedback will come in the form of video feedback in a screencast.

2. The student providing the feedback will find the shared document in his or her Google Drive account.

3. By tapping on the *i* icon, or the inspector, the student providing peer feedback can then export the Google Document using the Open in function.

Once the document is processed, the student providing peer feedback selects Explain Everything as the end location of the file. Once students have provided access to each other's versions of their papers, it is time for screencasting their peer feedback, which is done as follows:

1. They export the Google document from Google Drive and import it into Explain Everything. Then they press Record and provide audio feedback with ink or highlighted annotations while recording. The process is diagrammed on the EdTechTeacher screen in figure 3.8.

2. Once the screencast is complete, they export it from Explain Everything directly into Google Drive as either a Project file (which can only be viewed in Explain Everything) or a Video file (which can be viewed on any device).

3. Once the file is uploaded, the student who created the screencast shares either the Project file or the Video file from within the Google Drive app to the student who created the rough draft.

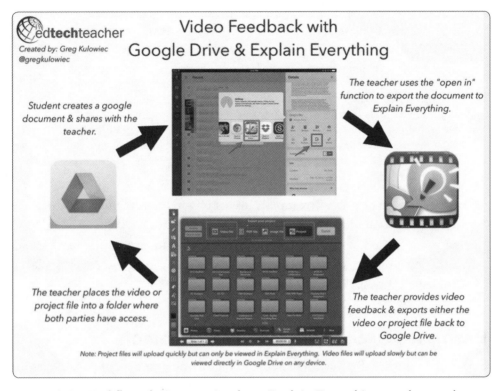

Figure 3.8: Workflow demonstrating how Explain Everything can be used to create video commentary on student papers.

Willingness to Learn Alongside Students

While teachers have a natural inclination to want to control everything that happens in the classroom, oftentimes the best learning environments for student creation allow space for inventiveness while encouraging teachers to learn alongside students. As Apple educational evangelist Don Orth (2013) points out:

> When students and teachers learn iPad tools together, the result is synergistic. In successful iPad Classrooms, teachers give students the space to demonstrate their work and understanding using a range of tools beyond just "a PowerPoint to show what you know about the Roman Empire" or "a five-hundred-word essay about the pros and cons of Communism." To paraphrase Chris Lehman (@chrislehmann), if we give students an assignment that produces twenty-five copies of identical work, we've given a recipe, not a thought-provoking opportunity for

growth. When teachers give some prompts to the unknown, and task students to show their deep understanding of a subject or skill with the best tools available, you might say miracles happen. We should be a little less afraid of miracles.

Who would have ever known that Rachel was an artist and could design an animation of the Golgi apparatus in action? Who would have guessed that Janet knew math fractions so well that her articulate screencasts could be used to teach other students in the grade above her?

If administration and faculty challenge students to do their best, and follow their natural inclinations and curiosity—to go outside the limited boundaries we set for the sake of standards—we open up a world of possibilities for students and for our society that adults might never imagine. I propose that we, as schools, challenge ourselves. I propose that we reexamine the essentials and assumptions that have driven curriculum, the way that we think learning looks, and give students some choices about the how and the what that they engage in.

For students, the process of creation is just as important as the final product. We are most excited about design processes that are collaborative, transparent, and leave enough room for individual student creation in order to ensure that teachers are constantly learning and constantly challenged. Let's now look at some examples of what students are doing and creating.

Examples of Student Creation Projects

In the sections that follow, we offer a series of ideas and examples of possibilities for student creation projects. This part of the chapter is meant to be chock-full of ideas, but remember: we're not encouraging you to attempt all of these approaches in a single unit or even in a single year. Rather, we hope these examples inspire creative thinking, so that as you think about your own learning goals, you can't help but imagine the kinds of activities students can engage in to meet those goals.

Publishing

As mobile devices become more common and comfortable platforms for reading online, the tools for creating high-quality e-books have grown more powerful and easier to use.

Students can write and publish books in apps like Book Creator and Creative Book Builder. These apps publish student work as an EPUB file, which can be read in iBooks and other e-book readers. Students can translate their notes from a unit into a chapter and compile a book over the course of the year, or they can create a retelling of a story that they read in class. Whatever the more summative writing assignment might be, writing and publishing an e-book gives a student a way to create more formal documentation of his or her learning. In Dan Bowdoin's math class, students took notes on solving one-step equations and incorporated those notes into a published electronic book.

Creating an e-book on the iPad offers multiple possibilities for sharing intellectual work and ideas. Creative Book Builder and Book Creator are two apps that can export an EPUB file to iBooks, Schoology, Subtext, or Dropbox. Each of these apps gives students the option of adding text, images, videos, and/or audio into their e-books.

With all of these exporting options, students need to first determine what multimedia they're importing. If they are bringing in Google Drive documents and will have a text-heavy e-book, the Creative Book Builder offers better tools. The app also connects to YouTube, Vimeo, and the iTunes account in your iPad. If students are creating more image-heavy e-books, then Book Creator has a simpler layout that helps with visualizing the final project. Either way, a teacher can use these apps to share processes and projects in the classroom or to capture and publish ideas, images, and other content from a conference or class.

For students who want to create a scrapbook to demonstrate their learning, Skrappy is an app that allows you to create a digital scrapbook that incorporates images, video, text, clip art, and audio (which can be sourced from iTunes or recorded straight into the app). Students can even add web content to their project. If students have a blog on a subject, they can embed one of their posts directly into their scrapbook. Skrappy's export options are limited to PDF and email, making this app better suited for accompanying a small-scale project like a presentation than for a larger project that requires publication to a public platform.

An app that students can use to create pop-up books with their iPads is ZooBurst. For students who want to do digital storytelling, this app gives you the tools to have both the characters and the setting pop up along the story line, an engaging medium for retelling a story, process, or historical event.

Tutorials

One of the best ways for students to demonstrate their understanding of a topic is by teaching what they are learning about to others.

SnapGuide is an app that provides an easy framework for creating a how-to guide in which students articulate a step-by-step process. Originally designed for recipes, the app has room for one picture per step, which gives students a way to clarify the sequential order of the task at hand. Whether the lesson is technical (like on how to post a blog or how to sign into a particular platform) or metacognitive (like on how to organize a notebook or solve a difficult problem), students can create reminders for their own learning.

Inherently, screencasting serves to teach someone something. While Explain Everything is a more robust screencasting app, suited more for older students, ShowMe is much easier to use with a very clean interface that offers little distraction for the younger user. Once created, ShowMe screencasts are uploaded to its website, where they can easily be shared with a link or embedded code. While this app does not include as many functions as other screencasting apps, its ease of use makes it perfect for the elementary- or middle-school classroom. ScreenChomp is another app that offers a more visually appropriate interface for younger users, allowing students to incorporate pictures as the background when they begin recording. Its screencasts can be uploaded to the ScreenChomp website without an account and can be shared in a link, email, or tweet. Younger students can log their iPads in to a class or teacher ScreenChomp account so that their creations get published directly to their account at ScreenCast.com or ShowMe.com. Having a central space for all tutorials allows other students to learn from their classmates.

If students want to create an animated comic for a project, Animation HD is an app that uses stop-motion frames to create a video. Students can use each frame to show the evolution of a story and then hit play to see them all run together. At the end, they can export the video to the camera roll, and from there they can post it, upload it to YouTube, or export it to their teacher.

In the same line of stop-motion video, myCreate allows students to take a video or use multiple pictures to create a film. If they want to show the evolution of a war on a map, for instance, or illustrate a process on a whiteboard, or even map a story to translate into another language, this app provides easy access to one medium of video.

If students want to make a more formal video to show what they have learned, the iMovie app gives users all the tools they need to shoot, edit, and publish. The app comes with two different templates that students can use to make videos related to the content of their class.

The first template is the iMovie Trailers feature, in which users choose a genre—horror, superhero, or romantic comedy—and then fill in the provided spaces with their own video clips, text, titles, and music, all of which are automatically published as a polished final product. Students can use this feature to create professional-looking movie trailers based on the content they're learning about in class: they might make a love story between dendrites and axons, a horror story about Boston's great molasses flood, or any story they're interested in. This template provides students with a fun structure with which to make intentional choices about what content to include and how to construct the clips of that content. The second template that iMovie offers is a simple, blank template, into which students can insert images or videos taken in the app or from the camera roll. This "start from scratch" template allows for more variability in movie creation, depending on what students are constructing.

App Smashing

Greg Kulowiec began an iPad workshop by asking, "Why limit our students to one tool at a time?" He pointed out that most teachers have students work with one app at a time to accomplish one particular purpose. He stressed that there is, however, more power in combining student content from multiple apps, or "app smashing." In other words, by merging content created from different apps, students' creative learning possibilities can be increased.

With app smashing, students can create small pieces of content with various applications that can later be used to create larger multimedia projects. For instance, students might add a caption to an image of the Eiffel Tower with Skitch and save it and then import the edited image into a screencasting app, such as Explain Everything, where they might add audio to tell a story. Next, they could save the Explain Everything file as a movie file and import it into iMovie. In iMovie, they could edit the movie and add a title, transition effects, and music. Once saved, they can import the movie file into Book Creator and include it in a multimedia book about historic Paris. Whether smashing two apps or several, one of the ultimate goals of creating multimedia projects with app smashing is to publish the final product to the web. Whether the final product is a collaborative screencast, a multimedia e-book, or a video, students can easily publish their creation to the web—so that they don't have to let their content "die on the iPad."

The idea behind app smashing is that when you select apps to control the final destination of the content, that content can often be used in conjunction with other apps to make a more polished, advanced, and compelling story or message. Visit http://edtechteacher.org/tutorials/appsmash for an EdTechTeacher video tutorial on how to app smash using iOS 7 and later.

The process therefore begins well before students create content, starting in the thoughtful selection of applications to export the content to various locations, most importantly the camera roll. For instance, a video screencast created with Explain Everything can later be incorporated into a multimedia book in the Book Creator app by first exporting the video from Explain Everything to the camera roll. The process is diagrammed on the EdTech Teacher screen in figure 3.9.

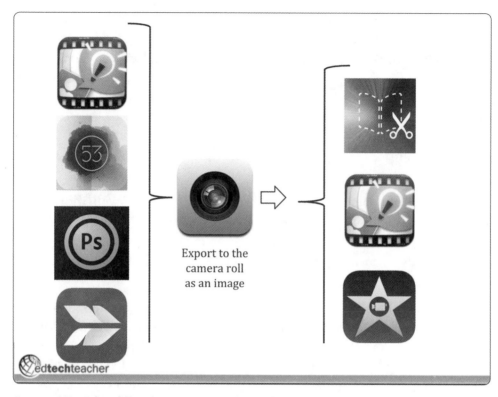

Figure 3.9: EdTechTeacher screen showing how video can be created and exported to the camera roll for final creation as an e-book, video, or screencast.

In a similar visual emphasis, but with more flexibility of text, *wet offers students a chance to make a step-by-step "recipe" of an event. Students can consider narratives (like, "How I learned to play the guitar"), explanatory text (such as, "How to overthrow a dictator"), or arguments (maybe, "How I'm a responsible digital citizen").

For an audiovisual presentation that features a speaking avatar, consider Tellagami. Tellagami is a free iPad app that features a speaking avatar that can read typed text or use a student's recorded voice. The speaking avatar can provide an explanation, tour, presentation, or other features on just about any topic. The topic can be featured in a background consisting of any picture the student chooses (the app pulls in pictures from the camera roll).

For a visual presentation that combines video and audio, PixnTell builds upon the same narrative form of beginning, middle, and end, but instead of just using static images, this app incorporates video clips. Students can record video with the app or shoot it ahead of time and add it from the camera roll. The element of video expands students' ability to teach the concepts they're studying. For example, if they're explaining how to stretch before exercise, they might take video clips of proper and improper techniques and explain their movements as they move along.

Posters and Images

Paper by FiftyThree is an elegant app that allows students to paint pictures and export them to the camera roll. This artistic app provides multiple brushes and a clean slate to paint on as well as a core palette of mixable colors and multiple styles of strokes to paint with. The app does not let the user zoom, providing a useful constraint when trying to capture an idea or image concisely. This is a useful app to use for creating base images, which can then be exported to the camera roll for further manipulation or use in other apps.

Many of the features of the mobile version of Photoshop look similar to the desktop version, providing an extremely robust app with which to create and edit images on the iPad. Without Photoshop experience, this app may be a bit overwhelming for some. However, it is extremely powerful and offers the unique feature of allowing users to layer multiple images together, allowing students to "mash up" images and then add text to create unique and interesting images. Once complete, images can be shared via Facebook or email or sent to the camera roll on the iPad. Due to its complexity, however, the Photoshop app is likely geared toward the advanced image editor at the high school level.

At a fraction of the cost, ArtStudio offers many of the advanced features of Photoshop Touch. This app allows you to select from a number of different drawing styles, colors, sizes, and opacities. Up to six layers can also be added within one image. This image-editing app is likely geared toward the advanced high school user. Exporting features include email, camera roll, and copy to the clipboard.

Students can also create posters using Explain Everything. This app enables pages to be exported as pictures and includes many tools for creating and editing images as well as for adding text and callouts.

If students have multiple images on one subject, they can use an app like PicStitch to collect the images into a single image. For example, if students are studying different types of leaves, they can choose a template that has four evenly sized boxes for four different leaf types they want to include. Or if they are studying the growth of a plant, they can select the Vertical Bars template to see the progress of the plant's growth over the four photos. An app like this one asks students to make selection choices, and then manipulate the images to create their desired effect. Constructing this visual narration, and having a product to return to, helps students in the process of their own learning.

If students need to make themselves a cheat sheet of a particular image or screenshot, they can use the Skitch app to create one. Skitch is the easiest app for creating and editing images and allows you to edit images from the camera roll, webpages, maps, and blank pages. Visit http://edtechteacher.org/tutorials/skitch for an EdTechTeacher video tutorial on editing images with the app. The interface is simple yet includes everything necessary for basic editing: line drawing, text boxes, arrows, and cropping of images. Students can choose from eight colors for drawing and easily adjust the width of the lines. Once complete, they can export images via Twitter or email or send them to the camera roll of the iPad. Skitch would be useful for students who need to remember the elements of a newspaper article (the headline, the byline, etc.), in that they could take the article photo, import it to Skitch, and use arrows and text boxes to label what they need to remember.

Visualize is an ideal app for making digital collages. The Gallery button provides a range of elements to begin a project with, and you can also import pictures from your camera. You can then add other elements, such as speech bubbles, shapes and arrows, icons and symbols, or frames, and elements can easily be resized and edited. Students could use the app to outline their writing process, construct a narrative to explain the most important facts about their current unit, or create a poster to study for the unit test. At the end of the year, they could flip through their series of "posters" and publish them to a class blog for an overall review. Then, they could save it back to the camera roll for easy reference.

Audio-Only Projects

Audio plays an important role in many of the projects that we've already discussed, and certainly many audio-only projects are worthy in their own right.

The iPad offers students various ways of capturing audio while listening to instructions or lectures. As previously mentioned, one easy method is for them to set up a SoundCloud account and save the clips they create during their classes for later. If they're already taking notes in Notability or Evernote, they can record an audio clip right into the note that they're writing.

Not only can students record their teacher and classmates, they also can record themselves. Sometimes, explaining things out loud is easier (and more helpful) than writing ideas down. If students hit Record and talk themselves through an idea for three minutes, they can later mine that brainstorming session for ideas while working on their final assignment.

If students want to create a compilation of audio clips, they can use GarageBand to do so. For example, if they're reviewing for a quiz and want to make an audio cheat sheet, they can edit together various clips they've recorded and create an MP3 track. This way, they can listen to it on the bus, on a run, or while doing chores at home.

Often, when preparing for a speech, or memorizing any information, it's helpful to listen to the words over and over. Students can record themselves reading the text out loud and then listen to it in order to commit it to memory. While some students may find it awkward to listen to themselves, this process can be helpful for calling attention to the little verbal errors one makes, like speaking too quickly, placing emphasis in the wrong place, or even just saying something that doesn't seem to ring true. Since they are the only ones listening to the recording, students are able to use audio as part of the polishing process.

In addition to creating audio for themselves to listen to, there are a multitude of ways that students can make recordings for others. If students create a subject-specific song and record it with SoundCloud or GarageBand, they can upload it through those accounts and then share it with their class. If they have a shorter clip, they can use the app Croak.it! to generate a web link, which they can then submit to their teachers in a Google Form.

If students want to create a longer audio piece—say a radio theater or a soundtrack for a silent video—they can use GarageBand to integrate the clips, add other music, and edit it all to sound exactly how they want it to. Uploading the final product through a teacher account makes it easier to access, as all of the assignments are centralized into one place. The same concept works well for turning in student work via SoundCloud: if students leave class to record themselves on their teacher's device (or if multiple devices are signed into the same account and students are recording concurrently), everything syncs immediately with the teacher's account.

The ease of compiling simultaneous multiple recordings makes constructing a multipart audiobook a simple process. For example, if at the end of a play, the teacher wants students to reduce a certain set of scenes to the most important parts, they can spend a few class periods on that work, and on the final day, all the groups can record at the same time. There is no waiting for access to just one microphone. SoundCloud offers easy access to embedding code, so teachers can take the freshly recorded clips and embed them on the class blog.

Students can also use SoundCloud to embed clips on their own blog. If they have constructed a transcript or conducted an oral interview, for instance, they can write out the text and include the embedded audio on their blog. This provides an opportunity for them to utilize the same knowledge in two different mediums, or use the writing as a form of metacognition of the oral project. They might also group up and stage a radio show, complete with different ambient or pertinent sounds, to demonstrate their understanding of a scene or excerpt. Embedding the clip on their blog or wiki encourages informative writing, which is useful in supplementing the multimedia with contextual text.

Teachers as Creators

Throughout this chapter, we've focused on students acting as creators with iPads, and we think that's the right place to start. Ultimately, our focus should be on what we as educators can empower in our students.

One way to empower students is through our example as educators. So we end this chapter with a whole series of ideas for how teachers can create media for their classroom or colleagues. Again, we hope the focus here will be on inspiring students, rather than simply creating materials for students to consume.

Jen Carey (2013), a school tech integrationist in Florida, outlines her thinking process in approaching iPads:

> As an educator, when I am given a new tool my first thought is "How can I use this in the classroom? How will I roll this out?" However, I have learned over the years that I need to pause, step back, and think, "Okay, how is this tool going to make my life and job easier? How can I use iPad to make me a better teacher?" Before I rush ahead with how I am going to roll out this device in my classrooms, I need to effectively incorporate it into my life and figure out how to use iPads to make me a better teacher.

Teachers go to conferences and take notes; they synthesize current events or classroom events and write blog posts; they write lesson plans, unit plans, and curriculum documents. For teachers, creation is about improving their practice or helping others improve theirs. With iPads, teachers have the on-the-go flexibility to create for themselves and to share with others.

Creating Images and Demonstrations

Teaching often happens through demonstration, and the iPad is uniquely equipped to create powerful visual lessons. Whether it be through static images, screencast tutorials, or short videos, teachers and students alike can leverage the power of the iPad to teach and learn through images.

One way that teachers can leverage this type of visual learning is with classroom images: pictures of the classroom setup, student work, whiteboards, or even sketches of how they teach a particular unit. These images, whether centered around students or personal processes, give glimpses into the usually shut-off environment of an individual classroom.

If teachers want a quick way to make a digital poster, Visualize is an easy tool to use. With Visualize, teachers can create custom images and infographics right on their iPad. This app includes every possible element necessary for the creation of thorough infographics: text, background images, cutout images, and so on. A unique feature of the app is that it allows images to be cut out from the original image, imported, resized, and rotated within a project. The app can easily be integrated across disciplines and grade levels, as the control features are extremely intuitive. If a teacher wants to highlight the classroom library, he or she can take multiple pictures, add a few bullet points of popular titles, and then export the images to their blog as a sort of advertisement of the space. Once a project is complete, Visualize has exporting options that allow users to send their work to the camera roll, email, Facebook, Picasa, or Dropbox.

If teachers want to create a tutorial on how they teach a particular process in class, they can use Explain Everything to walk through the process. With this app, you can insert pictures from a live shot, the camera roll, or a cloud-based account. When the screen is full, you simply insert additional slides. You can then have recording enabled while moving through multiple slides. Explain Everything can be exported to a camera roll, or YouTube, which then can be embedded on a teacher blog or wiki or shared via social media. Visit edtechteacher.org/tutorials/drive-EE for an EdTechTeacher video tutorial on using Explain Everything in Google Drive as a workflow system.

Whether it be creating images or tutorials, it is essential that teachers share their professional practice with the broader community. When teachers learn from one another, they become inspired in their own classroom. As teachers engage in their own learning community, they model that expectation with their students. Teachers often have classroom routines or processes that stay consistent throughout the year. Using Explain Everything to capture those processes creates resources for students to return to when needed. Doing this type of archiving allows teachers to be more responsive to particular students, by having general instructions available for watching and rewatching when they need them.

For immediate classroom work, teachers can use simple screencasting tools like Educreations or ShowMe in order to create quick explanations of an idea or process. For example, math teachers can capture the way they solve an equation and then post it for student viewing. By accumulating many of these videos, teachers can create a classroom archive of resources for a range of units. Furthermore, students can use these videos as exemplars and add their own videos, creating a robust academic space that uses only the iPad and a screencasting app.

When teachers create images and tutorials for their classrooms, they should consider what type of intellectual work they want to model and archive. These screencasting apps can be especially powerful if teachers will be returning to a particular app at various points in the year, as they can establish a classroom norm around the type of teaching they model.

Sharing Teacher Practice

Having a bevy of recording devices in classrooms opens up many new opportunities for teachers to share their practice with their peers. Teacher talk is extremely powerful, yet most of this peer interaction takes place in the teacher workroom (casual/personal) or during meeting times (structured/formal). Rarely do teachers get to hear their colleagues' interactions with students. The iPad could be the means to share more teacher talk in unobtrusive yet powerful ways.

Teachers are putting up more and more example lessons on YouTube, Vimeo, and TeacherTube, and it would be easy for them to record audio as they walk around and conference with students. Simply by holding the iPad, they have a microphone within arm's reach, even if they have to put the device down on a desk. They can record how they talk to particular students, give feedback to groups, and introduce and conclude lessons—all slices of classroom life captured through observation. Recording these moments without the fuss of video equipment can be a powerful way to instruct new teachers on what to say as well as to give experienced educators a glimpse into another classroom.

The iPad also makes it easy to take audio snippets and meld them into a larger whole. In the same way as programs like RadioLab mix up the traditional radio show, teachers can put spotlights on their classroom talk and include sound bites of real examples. For a robust app that can handle both the recording and editing, it's hard to find anything better than GarageBand.

If teachers have audio clips they want students to be able to listen to both in class and at home, SoundCloud has a straightforward app that syncs with its online counterpart. Teachers can record themselves reading a children's book, an excerpt, or even instructions for an assignment. Language teachers can easily capture themselves reading a passage or teaching a new sound, and students can listen to it as many times as they need to. For those students who "just don't listen," SoundCloud provides an opportunity to let them listen again.

One of the challenges of integrating iPads into classrooms is the "walled garden" nature of the device. The rise of social media in classrooms—blogs, wikis, podcasts, and so forth—was easy to document because the products of those efforts found a natural home on the web. As a result, it was easy to see what other teachers were doing. With iPads, on the other hand, more of the learning process happens within apps that aren't designed to publish content to the web, and often getting things online involves two or three steps. As a result, it may potentially become harder for tablet-using teachers to share their practice, and there will be more reinventing of the wheel in classrooms around the world.

Fortunately, there are many educators and organizations active on Twitter working to share best practices. Many can be found by searching the "#ettipad" and "#ipaded" hashtags. If you're not on Twitter, simply go to http://search.twitter.com and search "#ettipad." The search will lead you to recent tweets by teachers, education technology specialists, and others who are involved in integrating iPads in education. You'll uncover many tech integrationists tweeting about activities, projects, and resources.

When we perform our understandings in public, we hold ourselves to a higher standard and create products that can be meaningful and useful to others. We hope that educators will support and encourage students to publish books, tutorials, and other media on the web, and the best way to start is for teachers to model their own practice of publicly sharing their professional products. We've all benefited from teachers who gave us tips, materials, and lesson plans to help us grow in our practice, and the more that the vanguards of teaching with iPads share online, the easier it will be for those who follow.

Conclusion

The skills that we most want today's students to learn—persuasive communication, collaboration, well-structured problem solving—are skills that cannot be assessed with simple tests. They need to be assessed as performances, where students demonstrate—ideally in public—their knowledge, skills, and understanding.

The iPad can be used as a notebook, e-reader, video player, or gaming machine, but we are most interested in the iPad as a portable multimedia creation device. Using it this way is made possible by its combination of a camera, video recorder, audio recorder, and such a large input screen that editing, remixing, and publishing can all happen on the same device. It has much (though not all) of the media production capacities of a laptop computer, allowing for very sophisticated creations, but it also has a small footprint, little weight, and an instant on/off capacity which means that it's easy enough to pull out for a quick photo or a snippet of audio recording. Teachers have often thought of media creation projects as summative assessments because of the "overhead" time of ramping up media production efforts, and tablets open realistic new possibilities for formative assessment through creation.

In this chapter, we've proposed a framework for thinking about creation projects where educators start by thinking about learning goals and then work with students to consider what kinds of media creations would allow them to demonstrate their understanding of those learning goals. We hitch the app (or suite of apps) to the goal, rather than selecting an app and then figuring out what to have kids make. We think the process of creation is just as important as the final product, and we encourage teachers to scaffold projects in ways that encourage collaboration in production and transparency in the process.

What this looks like in practice is loud and messy, as real learning often is. When students develop their understanding through production rather than consumption, they talk, move, collaborate, and surprise. Learning spaces filled with media production look less like traditional classrooms with kids in quiet rows and more like bustling creative agencies. In all of these ways, the iPad becomes more than medium and means together, more than the engagement and tools it provides. The iPad changes the way that students and teachers think about act of creation in the learning experience.

4 iPad Professional Learning: Envisioning Innovation

It was the end of an EdTechTeacher iPad workshop and participants were being asked to respond to the prompt, "I used to think . . . but now I think . . ." They summarized what they thought of the iPad as a teaching and learning device before the workshop began and what they were thinking now that the workshop was over.

"I used to think the iPad was terrible," explained one middle school social studies teacher. "I couldn't find a good Manifest Destiny app or a good Oregon Trail app."

She explained that by the end of the workshop, her opinion had changed dramatically: "I understand now that there is so much students can do with an iPad, so many ways I can put them in situations to learn."

It is our hope that by this point you have decided not to follow the path of many teachers and administrators (and even entire school districts) who see the iPad simply as a repository of apps for teaching content. Instead, we hope you see that the process of teaching with iPads is not about finding and mastering apps but rather about envisioning how the iPad can contribute to environments where students have multiple creative pathways to learning that are aligned with relevant educational goals.

Equipped with a consumption-curation-creation framework, great opportunities for active, immersed learning emerge when educators reflect on how a small suite of apps can support diverse student understanding. With a focus on the iPad's creative learning potential, educators can cultivate a small set of evergreen apps—non-subject-specific apps like Explain Everything, Book Creator, and iMovie—into almost limitless instructional possibilities throughout the year for speaking, writing, listening, drawing, annotating, curating, collaborating, sharing, and more.

So, how do we help educators envision instructional possibilities and innovate? How do we construct and implement professional learning sessions and programs for teachers and administrators that go beyond finding apps and instead focus on unlocking the iPad's creative teaching potential?

EdTechTeacher is deeply committed to nurturing creative learning environments where students are engaged in active inquiry, problem solving, and taking increased responsibility for their own learning. The creative and collaborative learning spaces that we envision—and work with schools and educators to realize—represent a fundamental shift from traditional instructional practice. Throughout the process of working with schools, we remind ourselves that at the heart of any educational reform is change in the instructional core. Infrastructure, hardware, and apps are important, but the fundamental measure of success is the impact on learning that comes from exchanges between teacher and student and student and student. It's not the device we are serving. So, it's worth repeating: Technology should always be in the service of learning.

There are powerful, immersive technologies in the hands of educators who use them in limited ways. Conversely, there are classrooms with only an old desktop PC that is incorporated wonderfully and creatively by teachers. Technology, in and of itself, doesn't necessarily change learning. For us, this means that the primary focus of any professional development related to technology must be educators' vision of things they can do with technology, not the technology itself.

In our view, effective professional development can take many forms. Ideally it should minimize dealing with the nuts and bolts and focus on reflection and pedagogy. This process takes time, not a few short hours or days, and requires a continuous investment throughout the school year and beyond. The key is facilitating collaboration and communication among educational peers and exposing them to successful reflection practices both inside and outside of the institution. If we help teachers interact and reflect, both on-site and online, we help them grow professionally.

In the remainder of this chapter, we close the book by sharing the most important things we've learned about creating meaningful professional learning experiences for educators. We start by describing the characteristics of EdTechTeacher workshops and then describe our year-long program, Teaching for the 21st Century. Our hope is that these models will inform and inspire you as you work with your own colleagues to put iPads into the service of learning.

Anatomy of an EdTechTeacher Technology Workshop

Very early on in the development of EdTechTeacher, we realized that standing at the front of a room for long stretches of time and conducting "click here with me" lectures was boring. Some participants raced ahead and got lost. Other participants fell behind and got confused. Progress was slow, and learning was dull.

So we developed what we refer to as a challenge-based model of teacher development. For us, a challenge is a set of ordered tasks arranged to slowly increase in complexity, ideally leading to a meaningful product. We don't explain step by step how to do everything; rather, we create a list of things to do in an order that makes developmental sense.

Here's an example: When Tom begins an introductory iPad workshop, he puts a warm-up challenge on the screen. An example from one of the workshops is shown in figure 4.1. In short, he asks participants to complete a few fundamental tasks in order to ensure they know some basic (and intermediate) iPad features. Instead of Tom "teaching" participants iPad features, he asks them to learn them on their own in twenty minutes.

iPad "Warmup" Challenge

1. View most recent applications
2. Search your iPad for apps, emails & content
3. Create a folder (for 2+ apps)
4. Take a picture (and email it if email is set up)
5. Take a screenshot (and email if email is set up)
6. Lock your screen orientation.
7. Swipe between recent apps with 4 fingers. Close app with 5.
8. Create a 20-30 second movie starring a colleague.
9a. Go to http://edtechteacher.org/ipads. Add to Home Screen.
9b. Copy 2nd sentence in paragraph. Open Notes app and paste into Note.
9c. Select sentence and "Speak" it. (Hint: "Accessibility")
10. Bookmark http://vimeo.com/edtechteacher as "ETT Tutorials" in an "ETT" folder.

Figure 4.1: Example of an EdTechTeacher workshop challenge.

Before we begin the workshop, we explain the structure of the challenges to the participants. In particular, we make sure they understand that the goal is for them to learn through exploration rather than through imitation. This can be hard for people who are more accustomed to learning through direct instruction, so we try to create an environment where everyone feels supported. Participants are placed in groups of three to four people to help one another. If groups get stuck, we encourage them to ask other groups for help. If groups finish early, we have them start wandering the room to help others out. Groups can feel free to ask Tom or other instructors for help at any time. If everyone seems to get stuck in the same place, we pause for a minilesson on a particular topic.

When the warm-up challenge is over, Tom begins a reflection period by asking the following questions:

- "Was it hard to take a picture?" (Usual answer: "No, it's easy.")

- "Was it hard to shoot the video?" (Usual answer: "No.")

- "Was it hard to take a screenshot?" (Usual answer: "Not really.")

Tom points out that these iPad features, and many others, are relatively easy to learn. Then, he asks a follow-up question:

- "So, how can these features help improve teaching and learning?" (Then he waits patiently for an answer.)

Many iPad features are intuitive, but understanding how to build effective instructional practices is not. Thus, reflection is crucial. While all the educators in the workshop could readily take a picture, shoot a video, and capture a screenshot, many initially struggled to envision the iPad's instructional possibilities. After a silence, followed by a few prompts, the participants were asked to think of their own instructional possibilities. In time, they came to realize that the camera, video, and screenshots could all be used effectively for formative and summative assessment. As some of them pointed out, these technologies can all help to capture exemplary student work (such as a great science lab) or an exemplary student performance (such as a kindergarten student sharing toys cooperatively). One teacher adeptly pointed out that a screenshot is a tremendous tool for capturing student progress on an activity at any point in the learning process.

During the warm-up session, and throughout the day, the primary focus isn't on mastering the iPad. It's on helping educators grasp instructional scenarios in a mobile, personalized, and differentiated learning environment. We feel the professional learning pathway to developing instructional possibilities is not a "click here like me" or a how-to approach. It is prompting educators to constantly rethink learning in the context of new possibilities.

Figure 4.2 breaks down the components of one of our workshop sessions. As the figure illustrates, EdTechTeacher workshop participants typically spend most of their time immersed in hands-on challenges when exploring a concept. At the heart of the process are exercises that put participants in an immersive and problem-based learning environment. Instead of taking a "here is how you take a picture" or "this is how you switch apps" approach (characteristics of passive training sessions), we challenge educators to actively learn as much as they can on their own.

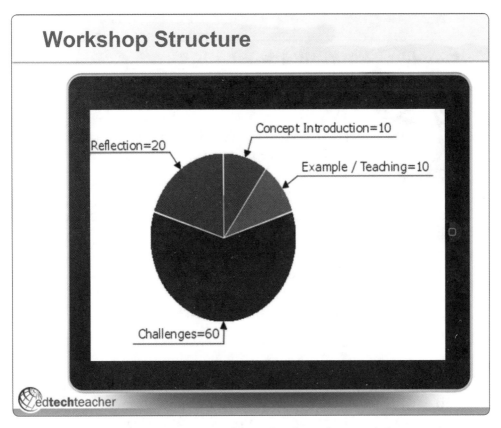

Figure 4.2: Individual components of an EdTechTeacher workshop session.

One of the benefits of challenge-based professional learning is that it averts contributing to a culture of dependency wherein teachers immediately turn to technology experts to show them how to do it. By completing even small challenges on their own, teachers gain a measure of confidence in their ability to tackle future challenges.

With apps specifically, we help teachers visualize new learning possibilities. For instance, we'll challenge educators to use an app to create a presentation, a tutorial, a short story, or a virtual tour. The following section explores our Explain Everything creativity challenge.

The Creativity Challenge: Explain Everything

In the creativity challenge, outlined in figure 4.3, we have participants get into groups and create a video that introduces people to some aspect of the neighborhood. We provide a few troubleshooting tips for the challenge but essentially send educators off to learn Explain Everything on their own by working together in small groups. We find that teachers can learn most of the features of this relatively complicated app, without intervention, in less than thirty minutes.

Explain Everything Challenge

<u>Within Your Group:</u>

1. Create a presentation that introduces people to some aspect of this area.

2. Consider what pictures and video you need to capture from around the building.
3. Snap photos and take videos (of locations, people, etc.)
4. Import images and videos into Explain Everything and use its creation and editing tools to make a brief "screencast" of 3-6 slides.
5. You have 30 minutes to complete the challenge!

Figure 4.3: Example of instructions for the creativity challenge in one of our workshops.

Throughout this challenge and others, we expect the participants to make mistakes and fail. During the thirty minutes they are exploring Explain Everything, participants will make a lot of mistakes. In many ways, learning technology is a messy adventure. They (and we) cannot anticipate every problem that might occur when using technology. Yet, in the end, we expect everyone to succeed. In our experience, every participant group has been able to solve problems and surmount obstacles to create a presentation demonstrating fundamental knowledge of Explain Everything features.

It's tempting for us to simply show teachers a whole lot about what they might do with an iPad or apps. Naturally, we do provide teachers with examples of what other teachers are doing with iPads (note that 10 percent of a particular session is usually dedicated to providing examples). However, at the same time, we try to nurture instructional creativity and not advance mimicry. When we show examples of what teachers can do with an app, they often mimic exactly what we just demonstrated. So, it's a matter of finding a balance between *showing* teachers what's possible and having them *discover* what's possible.

Leading With Pedagogy

Much like this book, our workshops move teachers through a consumption-curation-creation process of iPad exploration. When we broach apps, there is typically little demonstration or discussion of the app in question before we begin a hands-on challenge. Indeed, we try to deemphasize the app and instead focus on a pedagogical concept. For instance, we might introduce the Socrative instant response app this way:

> Wouldn't it be incredibly helpful if we could quickly know what our students were thinking, understanding, and feeling? And isn't the first step to becoming a better teacher getting to know our students?
>
> Imagine if we could instantaneously discover what our students know, understand, and feel while they are learning. If they were answering anonymously, what questions would you ask them? If they were identified, would you ask the same questions or different ones? What information could you solicit from them that could help your teaching? Which questions might be best served in the form of a quiz? Which might be best answered collaboratively in a group quiz?
>
> Would you just ask curriculum content questions, or would it help to know how they feel about other matters? If the latter, what questions would you ask? Which might be best answered anonymously? Armed with an instant knowledge about student understanding and opinions, how could we improve our teaching and better serve our students?
>
> So let's explore an app that can help us accomplish this goal.

In EdTechTeacher workshops, we attempt to lead with pedagogy and not a tool. Learning a tool is not our ultimate objective. So, we ask educators the same fundamental question in various ways: "What is it that you want students to be able to do?" Without a vision of what students can and will do, iPad integration lacks a clear purpose.

Six Workshop Characteristics

As much as possible, we design our professional development workshops to embody the characteristics of great classrooms. If we want teachers to integrate exemplary practices that will lead and inspire the next generation, then we must prepare them to do so in exemplary learning environments. To this end, we deliberately construct workshop environments that embody the following six characteristics.

1. **Constructivist:** EdTechTeacher workshops are marked by experimental learning. Participants actively discover the features, properties, and potentials of an app or a device. We challenge them to make sense of the tools for themselves. By not controlling how learners receive and process the information, we avoid positioning ourselves as the sole expert in the room. Instead, knowledge comes from everyone. To quote Harvard's David Weinberger: "The smartest person in the room is the room."

   In our workshops, we want teachers to fail early and to fail often. We want them to encounter stumbling blocks and obstacles and start developing the persistence and creativity to work through these challenges.

   Most trainings on school technology create dependency instead of empowerment. A typical workshop showcases an instructor at the front of the room who demonstrates a particular technology to participants. The participants may be sitting passively or simply duplicating the instructor's actions. At best, it's a "Do what I do" instructional strategy. Perhaps most relevantly, most workshops eliminate an environment where teachers learn through failure.

2. **Collaborative:** In our workshops, we encourage teachers to work collaboratively to uncover solutions to the challenges we provide. We want them to work independently of us and thereby gain some measure of confidence that they can solve future problems. We do not want to be the sole experts in the room. We do not want to control the knowledge. In the instructor-driven model, problems are often averted and participants don't develop the skills and persistence to troubleshoot and debug. In the collaborative model that we use, educators are working together, collaboratively, to make meaning and to help one another.

3. **Differentiated:** By providing both beginner and advanced challenges, we allow participants to work at their own pace, which we use as a model strategy for differentiated learning. We introduce apps that provide multiple pathways to learning. By providing access to varied tools, we attempt to give diverse learners varied ways of understanding and presenting content, while helping to ensure that we meet all of their needs. We also allow for differentiation of educational content as we ask various individuals to present content in different forms. Some teachers create virtual tours; other teachers create tutorials. Some of what they make is primarily visual, some is primarily auditory, and some is mostly text-based.

We often highlight the Explain Everything app in workshops because of its ability to provide multimodal pathways to understanding and to the presentation of knowledge and mastery. The goal is to help teachers create learning environments where diverse learners have varied opportunities to present what they know, what they understand, and what they feel. It is the versatility of this app in facilitating demonstrations of content mastery that's both appealing and useful.

4. **Personalized:** As instructors, we continually circulate the room during our workshops to provide just-in-time assistance and encouragement when needed. We work principally as facilitators instead of experts so as to foster a proper balance between self-exploration and direction.

   Additionally, we provide individual access to devices allowing for a more individualized educational experience. Since we do limited whole group instruction, we are now free to move about the room and engage students on a more individual and personal level, providing guidance and support. In this sense, the learning becomes less centered on the instructor and more focused on the participants.

5. **Mobile:** The Explain Everything challenge simulates a mobile learning experience for workshop participants. We hope it also serves as a catalyst for teachers to devise their own mobile learning experiences for students. A mobile device like the iPad adds a unique element to professional learning because it removes the limitations inherent in a classroom. No longer is the teacher the sole purveyor of information; rather, the students have a wealth, even a glut, of information available at their fingertips. They can now take that device (with its access, content, and materials) out of the classroom—on field trips, bus rides, the library, a park, home, and more.

6. **Goal oriented:** As much as possible, we try to structure our workshops around goals and challenges rather than repetition or emulation. After a brief introduction to a learning goal or tool, we give teachers the time and support to explore new tools and begin to develop lessons and plans for integrating technology in their own lessons. Participants spend their time exploring, playing, designing plans and resources for their own classrooms, and discussing new ideas with colleagues. By building learning spaces where participants can work toward creating meaningful products, we attempt to simulate the types of learning spaces we hope that teachers will emulate in their own classrooms.

SAMR Model

If you have spent any time at an educational technology talk or conference in the last few years, then you have no doubt been introduced to Dr. Ruben Puentedura's SAMR (substitution, modification, augmentation, redefinition) model of technological incorporation, as outlined in figure 4.4. We often use this model in the EdTechTeacher workshops as a way of helping teachers understand technology adoption as a developmental process.

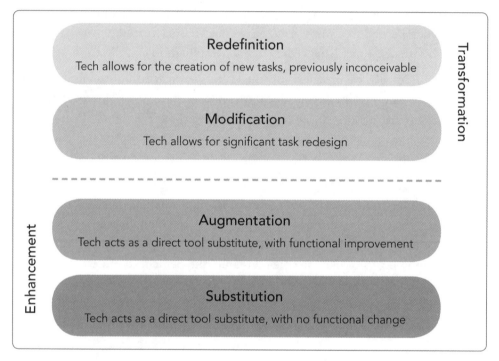

Figure 4.4: The SAMR model.

The SAMR model highlights four stages of technological adoption.

1. **Substitution:** Tech acts as a direct tool substitute, with no functional change (e.g., word processing). For instance, an annotation app can be used to highlight and underline words in a text document. Doing such an activity with technology is fundamentally an act of substitution, since highlighting and underlining words could be done with pen and paper.

2. **Augmentation:** Tech acts as a direct tool substitute, adding functional improvement to the basic tool (e.g., the spell check, thesaurus, and other tools in a program to enhance writing). An annotation app could also

provide functional improvement, or augmentation, to writing. Many annotation apps contain writing tools not available with pen and paper.

Certain activities transcend substitution and augmentation and could be classified as modification and redefinition. These activities fundamentally transform the activity.

3. **Modification:** Tech allows for significant task redesign (e.g., wikis or shared Google documents can be used to create a collaborative space). Students collaborating in an online writing space is an example of a significant redesign, or modification, of an activity.

4. **Redefinition:** Tech allows for the creation of new tasks that were previously inconceivable. Technology use can nurture new tasks, such as the creation of collaborative multimedia virtual tours that were not possible prior to it. One of the things we've seen about teachers and technology for nearly twenty years is that when exposed to emerging technologies, teachers tend to replicate existing practices. We've also known for a long time that many teachers go through a developmental process to get beyond extending existing practices. As the SAMR model describes, few teachers with access to new technologies will leap into imaginative new approaches. Rather, most of them will progress along a trajectory from the staid to the innovative.

The SAMR model is a useful reminder for teachers to examine their practices and ask in what ways they are merely using technology to gain small efficiencies in old practices and in what ways they are truly taking advantage of new possibilities.

Programs for Teacher Professional Learning: The T21 Program

While many institutions provide one day of professional development in education technology a year, the reality is that meaningful professional development must be ongoing and sustained. At EdTechTeacher, we encourage a blended instructional model, which includes on-site workshops, online modules, live webinars, and just-in-time support.

The Teaching for the 21st Century, or T21, program is a blended model of instruction designed for schools and districts to nurture leadership in education technology among a cohort of educators. Over the course of a year, EdTechTeacher leads three face-to-face professional development workshops, interspersed with online professional development training in the form of course modules and live webinars, as outlined in figure 4.5.

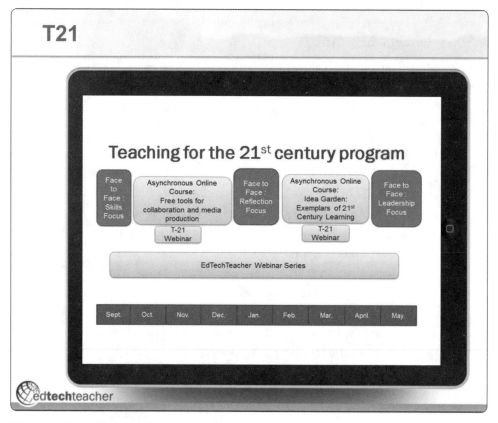

Figure 4.5: EdTechTeacher T21 blended, full-year professional learning program.

Part of the larger T21 program, the Nurturing the iPad Classroom program provides participants with a keen understanding of the iPad as a learning device, greater confidence in iPad knowledge and skills, practical activities for integrating iPads and educational apps in the curriculum, and a readiness to take leadership roles in promoting thoughtful technology use in classrooms.

The one-year program includes three main components:

1. **On-site workshops:** EdTechTeacher conducts three face-to-face day workshops throughout the year that open the door to new opportunities for teaching with iPads and support teachers in integrating technology as a regular, constant element of their teaching and classroom.

2. **Online modules:** We provide two six-week minicourses focusing on iPad integration and best practices that allow teachers and students to communicate, collaborate, and facilitate exemplary iPad integration. Each module takes approximately one hour to complete.

3. **Live webinars:** We facilitate two live one-hour webinars for participants and instructors to meet in a virtual room for live instruction, discussion, and feedback.

(For some schools or districts we design a "mini-T21," which typically includes one minicourse, one fewer workshop, and webinar.)

A T21 program includes an inaugural face-to-face workshop and kickoff of the program followed by the first six-week online course: Exploring iPad Apps and Web 2.0: Communication, Collaboration, Creativity, and Visible Thinking. The course introduces participants to apps and tools for communicating, collaborating, and creating with one another and making their thinking visible.

Topics include:

- **iPad as student response system:** Socrative
- **iPad as a digital notebook:** Evernote and Notability
- **iPad and creativity:** Explain Everything and Book Creator
- **iPad for collaboration:** Google Drive and Subtext
- **Structured and independent app research**

A module typically begins with a pedagogical concept, includes an introduction to a new app, a chance to try out the new app, and an opportunity to explore ways the tool might be useful in the classroom (the lessons are conducted asynchronously, so participants can complete their lessons at any point, and each is designed to take approximately one hour).

In the middle of this first course, EdTechTeacher holds a live webinar where participants meet online with an instructor to check on their understanding of the modules to date, add insights and more depth to module topics, and discuss classroom best practices. With a live webinar, along with email and telephone support, EdTechTeacher can provide sustained and just-in-time professional assistance to the educators it serves.

After the first course, participants meet with the instructor face to face for a second time. The second face-to-face workshop is followed by the second course: The iPad and Successful Classroom Integration.

Following are sample topics.

- **Specific classroom integration examples**
- **Reading strategies on the iPad:** e-books, PDF annotation, and voice/audio
- **Cloud computing and the iPad:** course content distribution strategies
- **iPad workflow solutions:** submitting and sharing work
- **SAMR:** moving iPad integration from substitution to redefinition

Like the first course, during the middle of this second course there are six modules and the cohort meets in a live webinar with an EdTechTeacher instructor. At the end of the course, the group meets again for another live webinar to check for understanding of progress and for a final, third face-to-face workshop. To end the program, participants develop an iPad-integration activity. Completion of all elements of the T21 program is a requisite for attaining three graduate credits.

A crucial component of the T21 model is the exchange of ideas among colleagues. We know that instructional practices are most acutely changed by peer-to-peer interaction, whether via a formal meeting or an informal encounter. National standards and administrative directives play an important role in shaping curriculum content and assessment, but changes in classroom practice are more directly influenced by exchanges with other educators. So the heart of every EdTechTeacher online module is collaborative exchange and discussion around metacognition and instructional practices. As part of the T21 program, we focus on ways that educators can connect, communicate, and collaborate with colleagues beyond their own institution. We work with them to develop a professional learning community of other educators and educational organizations who, like them, wish to continue learning and share ideas and resources.

Cycle of Experiment and Experience

If you read a dozen books on school leadership, you'll find that in many ways the basic ideas for transforming and improving schools are well understood. As leaders, we need to start by clearly identifying learning goals to target for improvement: communication, collaboration, creativity, and so forth. Next, we need to develop performance assessments so that we have a system for measuring the type of change we envision and hope to see. Then, we are required to develop instructional practices that facilitate the nurturing of desired competencies by providing professional development for teachers so that they can best prepare themselves and their students for the types of changes that will occur. Finally, we must evaluate student progress and revise our instruction accordingly, by taking the information we've gathered and creating system-wide instructional changes in order to help more students.

However, the progression from identifying learning goals to realizing systemic change is fraught with fears, difficulties, and obstacles. Not the least of the challenges is a cultural one. Many educators are skeptical of any new reform initiative, and rightly so. Many see reform in the classroom, technology infused or otherwise, as threatening their position and, at the very least, questioning of their performance and abilities. In the face of technology, there are those who are intransigent, or simply don't believe that any infusion of technology—at any point or any level—is a worthwhile undertaking. Thus, the success of any technology initiative depends on the coalescence of community support: between teachers, parents, students, staff, and others.

Teacher unease with technology is pervasive and takes many forms, which together constitute a significant impediment to effective technology integration. Teachers are concerned that technology will not work and may lead to a waste of time, and they often question its effectiveness as a replacement for traditional practices. They are often concerned that they won't know the technology as well as their students, and they fear that students may do or say something inappropriate with the technology. They worry about cyberbullying, cyberstalking, and other issues.

A major challenge for administrators is to encourage experimentation so that teachers and other educators in the community can work through their anxiety and gain an understanding of how technology can enhance classroom instruction. When teachers uncover innovative ways in which technology can engage students and nurture their essential skills and competencies, they start to move beyond the instructional practices that are ill suited to this new environment.

Effective leaders in school technology analyze instructional shortcomings, leave room for failure, and use that information to build institutional knowledge of best practices. They work to set teaching and learning priorities and point out how effective technology integration can support the institution's primary learning goals. They encourage faculty to collaborate and share their experiences. They alert others to shortfalls and ineffective uses and support faculty as they think more constructively and effectively about technology integration.

An institutional cycle of experimentation and reflection can reduce some of the individual or community fears about technology while building institutional capacity and growth. The cycle is diagrammed in figure 4.6.

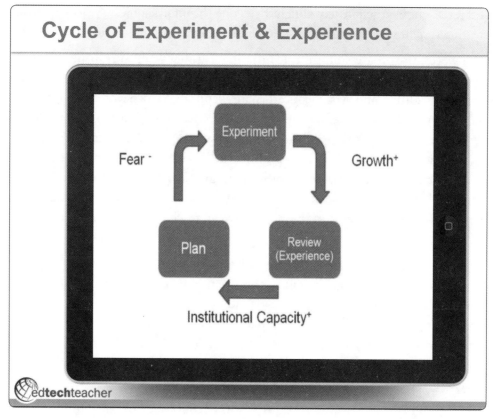

Figure 4.6: An institutional cycle of experimentation and reflection can reduce fears about technology while building institutional capacity and growth.

As teachers progress through this cycle, they gain increased access to an aggregated collection of lessons, strategies, tips, and resources created by their colleagues. These resources can help lessen some of their trepidation surrounding the use of technology, as they realize that they can turn to their colleagues—both in the building or at other schools and institutions—and move an entire community along an avenue toward increased experimentation.

The rub is that a cycle of experiment and experience will only be successful if tolerance of failure is part of the equation. Sometimes, it's only through making mistakes that teachers begin to really understand and recognize success.

Another specific way that administrators can nurture a culture of innovation is to create formal or informal "skunkworks," or groups of experimentation. Skunkworks are groups within an organization that are given special resources and protections that allow them to innovate and reshape the future of the organization. The purpose of the T21 program is to develop these kinds of skunkworks groups. These groups might either informally congregate to discuss best practices and strategies for using technology in the classroom or be formally sanctioned by the administration to develop recommended strategies or tools to be shared with the faculty.

Administrators can encourage these skunkworks programs by providing educators with the planning time they need to discuss technology integrations, lessons, activities, and strategies or by designating individual time to experiment with and share new technologies and their incorporation. Administrators can also help by providing professional development, either by hiring external consultants to provide "lessons learned" or strategies developed at other schools or by encouraging teachers to attend conferences, edCamps, online webinars, seminars, and other types of professional learning events. In fostering a culture of supported innovation and experimentation, each failure can be seen as some level of success for the learning and institutional knowledge that it creates.

Conclusion

Historically, the most exciting educational technology innovations have happened in pockets rather than whole communities. Nearly every school district has a few amazing teachers doing incredible things in pockets of excellence, but very few schools can claim that a new technology has substantially empowered new teaching practices throughout a community. Adapting to the new opportunities of mobile technologies is an incredible challenge, and it's one that requires whole faculties of educators to truly take advantage of.

In a community iPad undertaking, there should be an attempt to create a culture of innovation across school administrations, IT departments, and classroom teachers. Schools need to develop a clear understanding of the mission of technology as it pertains to the service of learning. The constituents need to be pulling together so that they can gather all of the infrastructure, professional development support, resources, and best practices available to them to ensure that their technology program is purposeful and effective.

We're excited about the possibilities that mobile devices, and especially the iPad, bring to classrooms. We hope that you have found our vision of a journey from consumption, through curation, to creation to be a compelling one. In the end, it's not about getting the right device or the right app. It's about communities of educators thinking deeply about what challenges the future holds for young people and then courageously examining how our classrooms and schools need to be reimagined to prepare our students for those futures.

References

Carey, J. (2013). How to use iPads for personal professional development. *Indiana Jen*. Retrieved from http://indianajen.com/2013/08/01/how-to-use-ipads-for-personal -professional-development/

Cowan, M. (2011). *Microbiology: A Systems Approach*. New York: McGraw Hill.

Darling-Hammond, L., Rosso, J., Austin, K., Orcutt, S., & Martin, D. (2015) Session 1: How people learn: Introduction to learning theory. The learning classroom: Theory to practice. Retrieved from http://www.learner.org/courses/learningclassroom/support/01_intro.pdf

Forston, K. (2013, Mar 13). The iPads in education conference that's not about iPads. *T.H.E. Journal*. Retrieved from http://thejournal.com/articles/2013/03/13/the-ipad-in -education-summit-thats-not-about-ipads.aspx

Gardner, H. (2011). *Truth, beauty, and goodness reframed*. New York: Basic.

Holland, B. (2012). What You Can Actually DO with an iPad. *EdTechTeacher*. Retrieved from http://edtechteacher.org/what-you-can-actually-do-with-an-ipad-from-beth-on-edudemic/

Jenkins, H. (2009). *Confronting the challenges of participatory culture: Media education for the 21st century*. Cambridge, MA: MIT Press.

Krathwohl, D. R. (2002). A revision of Bloom's taxonomy: An overview. *Theory Into Practice*, *41*(4), 212–218.

Kulowiec, G. (2014). iPads are like hammers. *EdTechTeacher*. Retrieved from http://edtechteacher.org/ipads-are-like-hammers-from-greg-on-edudemic/

Levy, F., & Murnane, R. J. (2014). Dancing with robots. *Third Way*. Retrieved from http://content.thirdway.org/publications/714/Dancing-With-Robots.pdf

McCusker, S. (2013). Four ways to ensure students are learning while creating. *Edudemic*. Retrieved from http://www.edudemic.com/learn-while-creating/

Orth, D. (2013). The role of student choice in connected classrooms. *EdTechTeacher*. Retrieved from http://edtechteacher.org/the-role-of-student-choice-in-connected-classrooms -from-don-on-edudemic/

Paper, S. (1980). *Mindstorms: Children, computers, and powerful ideas*. New York: Basic.

Reich, J., & Daccord, T. (2009). Designing student centered learning projects with Shneiderman's Collect-Relate-Create-Donate framework: The day in the life of a teenage hobo project. *Social Education*, *73*(3), 140–146.

Rheingold, H. (2012). *Net smart: How to thrive online*. Cambridge, MA: MIT Press.

Shneiderman, B. (2003). *Leonardo's laptop*. Cambridge, MA: MIT Press.

Sweeney, S. (2011, May 12). Truth, beauty, goodness. *Harvard Gazette*. Retrieved from http://news.harvard.edu/gazette/story/2011/05/truth-beauty-goodness/

Wiske, M. S. (1998). *Teaching for understanding: Linking research with practice*. San Francisco: Jossey-Bass.

Index